A History of PITTSBURGH Jazz

A History of PITTSBURGH *Jazz*

SWINGING *in the* STEEL CITY

Richard Gazarik and Karen Anthony Cole

Published by The History Press
Charleston, SC
www.historypress.com

First published 2021

Manufactured in the United States

ISBN 9781467144292

Library of Congress Control Number: 2020945735

Notice: The information in this book is true and complete to the best of our knowledge. It is offered without guarantee on the part of the authors or The History Press. The authors and The History Press disclaim all liability in connection with the use of this book.

To
David Cole and Lucy Gazarik

CONTENTS

ACKNOWLEDGEMENTS

It may take a village to raise a child, but it also takes a village to write a book. This work couldn't have been completed without the assistance of a number of people in Pittsburgh's jazz community whose contributions made this book possible. Marty Ashby and Mark Jackovic of the Manchester Craftsmen's Guild were generous with their time in allowing us to read the transcripts of interviews with musicians who were a part of the guild's oral history collection and featured in the film *We Knew What We Had: The Greatest Jazz Story Never Told*. The documentary details the musical talent and social factors that made Pittsburgh a pivotal player in the jazz culture of the United States. We also are grateful to Tim Wilson of the Music Department of Carnegie Library in Pittsburgh for his help in providing recordings of interviews with the city's jazz artists contained in the Maurice Levy Oral History Collection. We also are thankful for interviews with Dr. Nelson Harrison, Frank Cunimondo, Don Aliquo Sr. and Paul Thompson. We owe special thanks to Dr. Harrison and Mark Despotakis who reviewed the manuscript for errors and provided a number of photographs of some of the city's jazz greats. Tad Hershorn of the Institute of Jazz Studies at Rutgers University obtained documents from the Wilma Dobie Papers and granted us permission to quote from the records. Thanks to David Grinnell, coordinator of archives and manuscripts at the University of Pittsburgh Library System. Thanks also goes to our editor J. Banks Smithers for his support and encouragement.

There hasn't been a definitive book written on the history of jazz in Pittsburgh—and this work is by no means an attempt to accomplish that feat—but we hope it provides a starting point for an examination into the city's rich musical history and the artists who made it possible.

INTRODUCTION

Pittsburgh's industrial history is well documented, but the history of jazz in the city by the three rivers has been overshadowed by the musical legacies of New Orleans, Kansas City, Chicago and New York. Still, "molten hot music pours out of the blast furnaces of Pittsburgh's musical culture," notes the website Pittsburgh Music History.

Jazz still flows from Pittsburgh, which continues to produce young artists. The city's universities—Pitt, Carnegie-Mellon and Duquesne—turn out budding musicians while the Manchester Craftsmen's Guild and the African American Music Institute nurture young talent while keeping the jazz legacy of Pittsburgh alive.

In 2018, the Manchester Craftsmen's Guild produced *We Knew What We Had: The Greatest Jazz Story Never Told*, which appeared on public television stations across the country and features Pittsburgh artists who became famous. Ahmad Jamal, Art Blakey, Billy Strayhorn, George Benson, Erroll Garner and Earl "Fatha" Hines began performing in the Hill District, North Side and East Liberty neighborhoods before finding fame elsewhere. Other local musicians didn't attain individual fame but achieved success by playing in major bands and orchestras. Clinical psychologist and trombonist Dr. Nelson Harrison, saxophonist Grover Mitchell and trumpet player Al Aarons all played with Count Basie. Documentary filmmaker Ken Burns ignored the city's contributions to the genre in his 2000 series, *Jazz*, much to the chagrin of older musicians, who were angry about the snub.

Cover and program pages showing Pittsburgh musicians at a performance. *Erroll Garner Archive, University of Pittsburgh Library.*

Jazz is believed to have originated in New Orleans and evolved from a blend of African, French and Latin musical styles that became "American classical music," wrote Dr. Billy Taylor, a jazz pianist, broadcaster and educator, in his doctoral dissertation at the University of Massachusetts.

The city's jazz history was written by Black migrants who fled the South, leaving behind the hard life of sharecropping, violence, lynching and a caste system known as Jim Crow that forced Black people to live in a world apart. These migrants brought their families, their culture and their music on trains, in cars and horse-drawn carts and by foot to Pittsburgh—what they thought would be the "Promised Land."

When the migrants traveling by train crossed the Mason-Dixon line, they fell to their knees singing and praying, but their rejoicing was short-lived at the first glimpse of the city. They quickly realized it was not the "land of milk and honey" they expected. Instead, they found skies filled with smoke and steel mills belching fire so bright that it turned night into day. They were no longer in the sunny South but in a region surrounded by industry and a ravaged landscape.

Dust covered the ground like snow. Dust and grit enabled a person to taste the city in every breath. Adding to the pollution was smoke and odors from coking plants, glass factories, electrical plants and machine factories, according to Peter Gottlieb's *Making Their Own Way: Southern Blacks' Migration to Pittsburgh, 1916–1930.* Many Black sharecroppers found refuge in Pittsburgh's Hill District and work at the Black Diamond Steel Works, Solar Iron Works, Carnegie Steel Company, Jones & Laughlin Steel Company, Edgewater Steel, Crucible Steel, Mesta Machine and Union Switch & Signal, according to Jazz Age novelist Erskine Caldwell, who attacked poverty, racism and sharecropping in his book *Tenant Farmer.*

They also learned that the caste system they fled north to escape existed in Pittsburgh, one of the most segregated cities in the nation at the time. Migrants referred to Pittsburgh as "up south," a reference to the detested racial system of Jim Crow that existed in the city. Newly arrived Black residents were greeted by racial epithets, discrimination and

Kelly's Bar at the corner of Fifth and Wylie Avenues was one of dozens of places where a person could listen to jazz. *Pittsburgh City Photographer Collection, University of Pittsburgh Digital Library System.*

humiliation. Finding a decent place to live in the slums of Pittsburgh was nearly impossible. The migrants learned that the city was no different than southern states in terms of attitudes and behavior, wrote Dr. Janelle R. Carter in her 2015 doctoral dissertation at Duquesne University, "From Their Own Voices: The Lived Experiences of African Americans Exposed to Jim Crow."

"I first came to Pittsburgh…cause I knew down south was prejudiced but up here I didn't. I had no idea it was prejudiced," said one migrant interviewed by Carter. The African music style survived the trek north and helped blend European classical music and African music into what we now call jazz.

Pittsburgh is reviving its musical culture. In 2018, the *Pittsburgh Ecosystem Study: Activating a Community Response* was designed to offer recommendations to make the city a music destination and create a thriving music industry to support musicians. Musicians have fallen on difficult times because music, particularly jazz, is not viewed as an industry. Of the 1,800 respondents surveyed by Sound Music Cities in Austin, Texas, the consulting firm that compiled the report, 59 percent had full-time jobs other than in music; 59 percent made less than $10,000 a year making music; 85 percent financed

View of Centre Avenue in the Hill District. Rosen's was another venue where people gathered to listen to live jazz. *University of Pittsburgh Library System.*

their musical careers out of their own pocket; and 25 percent had two or more part-time jobs to survive.

Pittsburgh once was filled with clubs and bars that featured jazz. The music was so popular that it was estimated that thirty-five thousand people a week went to places that offered jazz, according to a booking report at the Carnegie Library in Pittsburgh. Younger people no longer embrace jazz in the way earlier generations did.

1

PITTSBURGH'S LOVE AFFAIR WITH THE PIANO

The Pittsburgh music world is diverse. The city and southwestern Pennsylvania have produced scores of noted musicians, singers, musical groups and composers in jazz, classical music, pop, rock 'n' roll, blues and hip-hop. In jazz, Earl "Fatha" Hines, Erroll Garner, Mary Lou Williams, Roy Eldridge, Ray Brown, Billy Eckstine, Billy Strayhorn, George Benson and Ahmad Jamal began their careers in Pittsburgh.

Classical pianists Earl Wild, Norman Frauenheim, Beveridge Webster, Paul Wilson and Patricia Prattis Jennings and violinist Paul Ross became the first Black musicians to join a major symphony when they were hired by the Pittsburgh Symphony in the mid-1960s. Byron Janis was born in nearby McKeesport, and Antonio Modarelli came from nearby Braddock.

The world of pop music claims Bret Michaels, formerly of the group Poison. Donnie Iris sang with the local band the Jaggerz and Christina Aguilera was named by *Rolling Stone* as one of the "100 greatest singers of all time." The list of singers from the region includes Jackie Evancho, Eddie Jefferson, Maxine Sullivan, Tiny Irvin, Phyllis Hyman, Vivian Reed, Florence "Gail Sonders" Davis, Shanice Wilson, Yolanda Barber, Sandy Staley, Michele Benson, Billy Porter, Maureen Budway, Lenore Nemetz, Perry Como, Bobby Vinton and singing groups Rusted Root, Tommy James and the Shondells, the Jaggerz, Skyliners, the El Vinos, the El Capris, the Laurels, Marcels, Del Vikings, Chuck Jackson, Adam Wade, Marva Josie, Lou Christie and the Vogues. Blues artists are represented by king of boogie-woogie Pine Top Smith, violinist Papa John Creach of Jefferson Starship and singer Chizmo

Charles Anderson. Composers include Billy Strayhorn, Henry Mancini, Sammy Nestico, Melvin and Mervin Steals and Billy May. Hip-hop is represented by Jasiri X, Wiz Khalifa and the late Mac Miller and Jimmy Wopo.

George Benson played on Hill District streets for pennies until he was hired to perform as a child at the Café Paris. His stay there ended in a police raid that landed him in reform school. *Courtesy Wikimedia Commons.*

It was musicians from the Pittsburgh school of piano jazz that put Pittsburgh on the musical map. Strayhorn, Garner, Hines, Williams, Horace Parlan, Jamal, Walt Harper, Alyce Brooks, Reid Jaynes, Michael "Dodo" Marmarosa, Frank Cunimondo, Linton Garner (the brother of Erroll Garner), Johnny Costa, Charles Bell, David Budway and Sam Johnson all hailed from the city. They paid their musical dues amid the cigarette smoke, scent of stale beer and twinkling ice cubes in the city's tightly packed and sweaty boozy clubs and cabarets. Some achieved sought-after fame, like Garner, Jamal, Hines and Williams, while great artists such as pianist Sam Johnson, Carl Arter and Robert Head fell into obscurity despite being held in esteem by their fellow musicians.

Pittsburgh has had a long-standing love affair with the piano ever since Charles Rosenbaum began building them in the city in 1812, when he opened a factory. He advertised pianos for sale in the *Pennsylvania Weekly Gazette* in 1814. Henry Kleber later imported pianos from eastern Pennsylvania after he opened a store in 1846.

"Pittsburgh rivaled New York City in its development of the piano in jazz.... Pittsburgh's involvement with the piano was a major cultural phenomenon stimulated by the Great Migration's thirst for cultural advancement and the traditional respect accorded to harmoniums and pianos in southern black life," wrote William Howland Kennedy in *Jazz on the River*.

Sam Johnson was one of the least known but most talented pianists ever to come out of Pittsburgh according to his friend Nelson Harrison. Johnson was best friends with Erroll Garner. They were both self-taught and sometimes played at the same clubs and learned techniques from each other said Harrison. Johnson was the pianist in the late 1940s for a local group, the Four Strings, that included violinist Joe Kennedy Jr. and later a fourteen-year-old Ahmad Jamal. "He was a marvelous reader at that young age," Harrison recalled. The group played at clubs around the Pittsburgh, and when Mary Lou Williams heard them, she arranged for them to record on the Asche record label in 1947. The Four Strings performed in Chicago, and there Jamal stayed to begin his musical career.

Perhaps one of the most talented artists to come out of the city was Strayhorn, who was composing sophisticated music at sixteen. While attending Westinghouse High School, he wrote a Gershwin-esque musical for a school production, *Fantastic Rhythm*, that comprised ten original songs.

Billy Strayhorn became Duke Ellington's alter ego in a collaboration that lasted nearly three decades. *Library of Congress.*

Roosevelt Theatre was a hotbed for jazz and attracted major orchestras. *University of Pittsburgh Library System.*

He also did the arranging for the instruments of a twelve-piece orchestra and wrote accompanying pieces for dances and skits. The musical was so successful that it was performed at the Roosevelt Theatre in the Hill District and at Black-owned theaters in Rankin, Braddock, Homestead and East Liberty.

These budding Pittsburgh-bred musicians were being exposed to the music of New Orleans via riverboats, vaudeville acts, blues artists and ragtime players. Because classical music, at that time, was a realm for white males only, these talented Black musicians gravitated to jazz.

Pittsburgh has also produced no shortage of bassists, including Ray Brown, Paul Chambers, Eddie Safranski, John Heard, David Izenson, Mickey Bass, Richie Goods, Jimmy DeJulio, Bobby Boswell and Lillian Carter, one of the few women instrumentalists to play in Pittsburgh jazz clubs. Boswell played with Chick Webb, Billie Holiday, Max Roach and Count Basie. Safranski played for Benny Goodman and Stan Kenton and was part of the orchestras that backed up Tony Bennett and Sarah Vaughan. Right behind the bassists are legendary drummers Art Blakey, Kenny "Klook" Clarke, Beaver Harris, Joe Harris, J.C. Moses, Billy James and Allen Blairman. Drummer Roger Humphries still performs in Pittsburgh along with Poogie Bell, Jeff "Tain" Watts and Tom Wendt.

Harris Theater, Duquesne Way looking northeast. The Harris Theater now is part of the Pittsburgh Cultural Trust. *University of Pittsburgh Library System.*

Trumpet player Roy Eldridge was born on Pittsburgh's North Side and was nicknamed "Little Jazz" because he was only five feet, six inches tall. He became the first Black musician to play in an all-white orchestra when Gene Krupa hired him. Babe Russin played saxophone for Glenn Miller, Tommy Dorsey and Benny Goodman. Bassist Wyatt Ruther, who played the double bass, backed up Dave Brubeck, Erroll Garner, Milt Hinton, Stan Getz and Chico Hamilton.

Eldridge was very competitive when it came to music. He always tried to outplay other trumpet players. In *Jazz Anecdotes*, Dizzy Gillespie said Eldridge would go to physical extremes before letting someone outplay him. One time, Gillespie and Eldridge were walking past a New York club, and Eldridge went in. Gillespie asked to perform first "cause when you get up to play you don't know how to act."

Eldridge did feel intimidated when he moved to New York because of the skill of other musicians. He recalled in *Jazz Anecdotes*, "These cats were playing so great and I was scared to death." His brother and another musician took him to a bar during an intermission, bought him several drinks to loosen him up and then returned to the bandstand. "By the time we got back on man, I was feeling no pain," he said.

Ray Brown grew up in the Oakland section of Pittsburgh and played with some of the greatest jazz groups of all time. He joined Snookum Russell's

Roy Eldridge was known as "Little Jazz." He became one of the first African American musicians in a white band when he joined Gene Krupa. *Library of Congress.*

band after high school and was hired by Dizzy Gillespie, sharing the same stage as Charlie Parker, Bud Powell and Max Roach, according to the *New York Times*. He joined the Oscar Peterson Trio and performed in all of Frank Sinatra's television specials. He has been ranked among the great jazz bassists Oscar Pettiford, Charlie Mingus, Milt Hinton and Jimmy Blanton, reported the *Times*.

Guitarists Ray Crawford and Joe Negri made names for themselves in the jazz world. Crawford started his musical career playing tenor sax and clarinet in a group led by drummer Art Blakey. He began playing in Pittsburgh and then performed with Fletcher Henderson's orchestra before he was sidelined by tuberculosis. Crawford switched to the guitar and became a member of Ahmad Jamal's trio.

Negri was the musical director for *Mr. Rogers' Neighborhood*, recorded an album with Michael Feinstein and later appeared at the Newport Jazz Festival. Pianist Johnny Costa developed a national reputation but returned to Pittsburgh to work for Fred Rogers on the same public television program. Negri, in an interview, said he walked into the Crawford Grill one night with George Benson, who already was a national star. Benson expected to be mobbed by fans, but it was Negri who was the center of attention. "That's Joe Negri," the crowd shouted. "They were all over Joe," Benson recounted in an interview with the Manchester Craftsmen's Guild.

Jimmy Ponder taught himself to play the guitar by ear practicing six hours a day. He went professional at eleven and was known for his grueling

Left: Bassist Ray Brown in background playing with Milt Jackson on vibes. *Wikipedia.*

Below: Guitarist Joe Negri had a nationwide reputation as a musician but was equally famous as Handyman Negri on *Mr. Rogers Neighborhood* on public television. *Wikipedia.*

work habits. He would play five hours a night at a club seven nights a week. Then he would perform at Sunday afternoon matinees and play five more hours in the evening.

Barry Galbraith was a little-known guitarist from Pittsburgh who built a big reputation in the jazz world playing with Claude Thornhill's orchestra and later with Babe Russin, Art Tatum, Red Norvo, Miles Davis, Coleman Hawkins, Oscar Peterson and Max Roach. He also accompanied singers

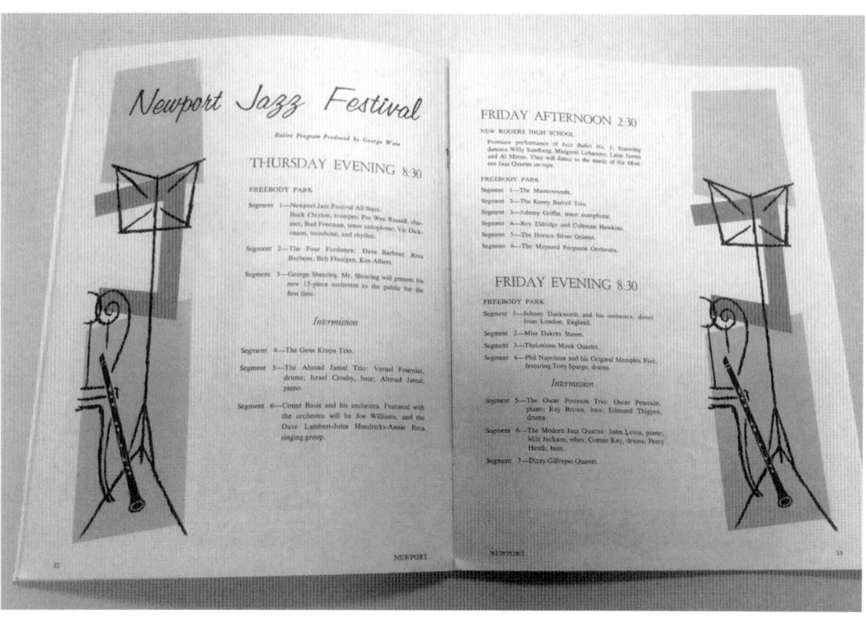

Newport Jazz Festival

Entire Program Produced by George Wein

THURSDAY EVENING 8:30

FREEBODY PARK

Segment 1—Newport Jazz Festival All Stars. Buck Clayton, trumpet; Pee Wee Russell, clarinet; Bud Freeman, tenor saxophone; Vic Dickenson, trombone, and rhythm.

Segment 2—The Four Freshmen: Dave Barbour, Ross Barbour, Bob Flanigan, Ken Albers.

Segment 3—George Shearing. Mr. Shearing will present his new 15-piece orchestra to the public for the first time.

Intermission

Segment 4—The Gene Krupa Trio.

Segment 5—The Ahmad Jamal Trio: Vernel Fournier, drums; Israel Crosby, bass; Ahmad Jamal, piano.

Segment 6—Count Basie and his orchestra. Featured with the orchestra will be Joe Williams, and the Dave Lambert-John Hendricks-Annie Ross singing group.

32 NEWPORT

FRIDAY AFTERNOON 2:30

NEW ROGERS HIGH SCHOOL

Premiere performance of *Jazz Ballet No. 1*, featuring dancers Willy Sandberg, Margaret Lithander, Leon James and Al Minns. They will dance to the music of the Modern Jazz Quartet on tape.

FREEBODY PARK

Segment 1—The Mastersounds.

Segment 2—The Kenny Burrell Trio.

Segment 3—Johnny Griffin, tenor saxophone.

Segment 4—Roy Eldridge and Coleman Hawkins.

Segment 5—The Horace Silver Quintet.

Segment 6—The Maynard Ferguson Orchestra.

FRIDAY EVENING 8:30

FREEBODY PARK

Segment 1—Johnny Dankworth and his orchestra, direct from London, England.

Segment 2—Miss Dakota Staton.

Segment 3—Thelonious Monk Quartet.

Segment 4—Phil Napoleon and his Original Memphis Five, featuring Tony Spargo, drums.

Intermission

Segment 5—The Oscar Peterson Trio: Oscar Peterson, piano; Ray Brown, bass; Edmund Thigpen, drums.

Segment 6—The Modern Jazz Quartet: John Lewis, piano; Milt Jackson, vibes; Connie Kay, drums; Percy Heath, bass.

Segment 7—Dizzy Gillespie Quintet.

NEWPORT 33

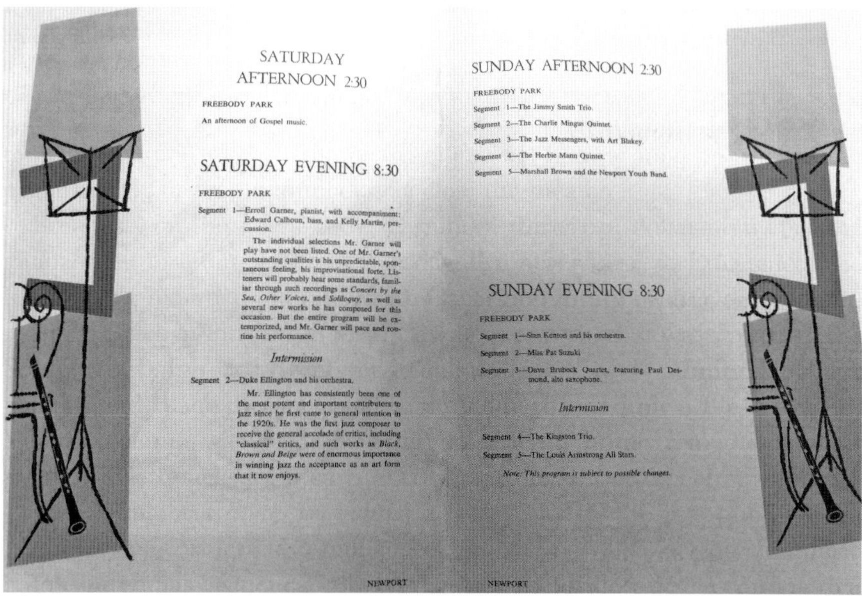

SATURDAY AFTERNOON 2:30

FREEBODY PARK

An afternoon of Gospel music.

SATURDAY EVENING 8:30

FREEBODY PARK

Segment 1—Erroll Garner, pianist, with accompaniment: Edward Calhoun, bass, and Kelly Martin, percussion.

The individual selections Mr. Garner will play have not been listed. One of Mr. Garner's outstanding qualities is his unpredictable, spontaneous feeling, his improvisational forte. Listeners will probably hear some standards, familiar through such recordings as *Concert by the Sea*, *Other Voices*, and *Soliloquy*, as well as several new works he has composed for this occasion. But the entire program will be extemporized, and Mr. Garner will pace and routine his performance.

Intermission

Segment 2—Duke Ellington and his orchestra.

Mr. Ellington has consistently been one of the most potent and important contributors to jazz since he first came to general attention in the 1920s. He was the first jazz composer to receive the general accolade of critics, including "classical" critics, and such works as *Black, Brown and Beige* were of enormous importance in winning jazz the acceptance as an art form that it now enjoys.

NEWPORT

SUNDAY AFTERNOON 2:30

FREEBODY PARK

Segment 1—The Jimmy Smith Trio.

Segment 2—The Charlie Mingus Quintet.

Segment 3—The Jazz Messengers, with Art Blakey.

Segment 4—The Herbie Mann Quintet.

Segment 5—Marshall Brown and the Newport Youth Band.

SUNDAY EVENING 8:30

FREEBODY PARK

Segment 1—Stan Kenton and his orchestra.

Segment 2—Miss Pat Suzuki

Segment 3—Dave Brubeck Quartet, featuring Paul Desmond, alto saxophone.

Intermission

Segment 4—The Kingston Trio.

Segment 5—The Louis Armstrong All Stars.

Note: This program is subject to possible changes.

NEWPORT

Programs for the 1959 Newport Jazz Festival featuring the Ahmad Jamal Trio, Roy Eldridge, the Horace Silver Quintet and Ray Brown in the Oscar Peterson Trio. *Erroll Garner Archive, University of Pittsburgh Library System.*

Singer Ann Baker was born south of Pittsburgh in Washington, Pennsylvania, and began her career singing with Louis Armstrong and performing in orchestras led by Count Basie, Lionel Hampton and Billy Eckstine. *Courtesy of Nelson Harrison.*

Anita O'Day, Billie Holiday, Sarah Vaughan, Dinah Washington, Ella Fitzgerald and Tony Bennett.

Trombonists Grover Mitchell and Nelson Harrison were members of the Count Basie Orchestra. Mitchell later led the band after Basie's death. Trumpeter Danny Conn backed up everybody from Frank Sinatra, Dean Martin and Sammy Davis Jr. to strippers Blaze Starr and Tempest Storm when he was a member of the house band at the former Casino Theater, a Pittsburgh strip joint. Robert "Cutty" Cutshall played trombone for Benny Goodman and Eddie Condon in the 1940s and worked with Ella Fitzgerald.

Dodo Marmarosa, who was born in East Liberty, toured with Tommy Dorsey, Gene Krupa and Artie Shaw and later recorded with Charlie Parker and Lester Young before becoming somewhat of a recluse and disappearing from the music scene.

Pittsburgh has produced no shortage of singers, including Lena Horne, who began her career in Pittsburgh; Maxine Sullivan; Dakota Staton; Ann Baker; Phyllis Hyman; and Delsey McKay, whose uncle Eddie Jefferson introduced vocalese to the singing world.

Despite its long musical history, Pittsburgh has been ignored by the jazz world. Documentary filmmaker Ken Burns never mentioned Pittsburgh and ignored Erroll Garner's contribution to the music in his miniseries *Jazz*. In a

Erroll Garner and his agent Martha Glaser. *Erroll Garner Archive, University of Pittsburgh Library System.*

piece Burns wrote for the *Los Angeles Times*, he said, "Great as Garner is, you don't want to take away space from a Charlie Parker or a Miles Davis or a Thelonious Monk to support somebody who wasn't a seminal inventor, even though he was very popular and did wonderful things."

Martha Glaser, Garner's longtime agent, was incensed by the omission. "The bleep has hit the fan re the Burns omission of EG from his magnum opus because Garner is not a seminal inventor and not an original and has no influence," wrote Glaser to Columbia Records producer George Avakian in 2001. She added a postscript: "I don't give a bleep that EG is not in Burns' marathon thing—I do care that Burns has the gall to DEFINE WHO GARNER WAS CREATIVELY AND HISTORICALLY."

The letters between Glaser and Avakian are contained in the Erroll Garner papers held by the University of Pittsburgh. Avakian also was angry about the slight. "Just as the stench of rotting sickies who don't realize that he was a genius will never go away, neither will the timeless creativity and originality of Erroll Garner."

Glaser wrote to the head of Burns's production company, Florentine Films, on June 12, 2000, that she would not allow Garner's iconic recording of "Misty" to be used in the series:

> *It is difficult for me to fathom how Mr. Burns and his staff and committee of jazz expert consultants would opt to omit Mr. Garner from the film series. Historical revisionism? Regarding your reference to MISTY—please do not even think of even using MISTY in your soundtrack or any part of your film/book project. Given the circumstances, MISTY would not be available for licensing or any use in your productions, including the present Ken Burn project.*

Erroll Garner performing on stage. Erroll Garner Archive. *University of Pittsburgh Library System.*

Garner caught the attention of the American public after performing on *The Tonight Show*, then hosted by Steve Allen. That led to appearances on shows hosted by Ed Sullivan, Jackie Gleason, Perry Como, Gary Moore, Andy Williams, Mike Douglas and David Frost. Garner's trademark tune, "Misty," has been recorded by a number of singers, and his live album *Concert by the Sea* recorded in Carmel-by-the-Sea, California, is heralded by critics as the greatest live jazz concert ever recorded.

Pittsburgh's jazz culture also has legendary history. Places like the Hill District, downtown, East Liberty and the North Side were filled with nightclubs and crowded every night of the week with people wanting to listen to good jazz. The most famous clubs were located in the Hill District, which overlooks downtown.

The Hill District was synonymous with music. "The Hill was a place with hundreds of venues committed to jazz....One could literally walk the street and hear the crying, loving sounds from the sax play," wrote Pittsburgh writer John Brewer Jr. in his book *Pittsburgh Jazz*. "Food joints, fresh with the smell of barbecue ribs, wings and fries, were served with jazzy sounds that made one happy to be alive and hanging out on Wylie Avenue in the Hill District." Nelson Harrison said the Hill never slept. People would be on the streets in the early morning hours buying barbecue that residents were smoking in their yards. In a personal interview, Harrison said wherever there were Black people, there was jazz.

The Hill District was the location for the famed Crawford Grill, the Musicians Club, the Loendi Club, the Bambola, the Savoy Ballroom, the Roosevelt Theatre, the Pythian Temple and the Elmore Theater, where Bessie Smith, Ethel Waters, Ma Rainey and Jelly Roll Morton once performed.

Crawford Grill #2. The grill, located in the Hill District, was a must stop for touring musicians in Pittsburgh. *Courtesy of Nelson Harrison.*

Wylie Avenue looking west. *University of Pittsburgh Library System.*

There also were a number of not-so-famous venues such as the Pitt Pot, High Hat, Mutt's Hutt and the Harlem Casino. Many of the legendary clubs were destroyed when the city embarked on an urban renewal project in the 1950s that saw the demolition of the lower part of the historic Hill District neighborhood, where many of the clubs were located.

Trombonist Grover Mitchell's neighbors in East Liberty were Mary Lou Williams, Billy Eckstine and Billy Strayhorn along with brothers Erroll and Linton Garner. He recounted in a 1994 interview with *Online Trombone Magazine* that some truly great musicians lived here who never achieved fame but were well known in Pittsburgh's highly competitive music circles. Mitchell said:

> *They had a great pianist that never quite made it. His name was Sam Johnson —a monster, a great piano player. He never gained any fame, but everybody from Pittsburgh knows him. Ray Crawford, the guitarist—he's from there. On and on and on. Competition was stout—you had to play pretty well in Pittsburgh. Pittsburgh was a mean town—a work town—so we had pretty good training from each other. And you were always doing something to "one-upsman" everybody else. You're so busy dealing with the competitive thing it either makes you or breaks you—in those days it did.*

Pythian Temple on Wylie Avenue was part of the Grand Lodge of the Black Knights of Pythias of North America. Harry Hendel purchased the building and renamed it the New Granada Theater and housed the New Savoy Ballroom in its ground floor. It was designed by Pittsburgh's first Black architect, Louis A. Bellinger, and was added to the National Register of Historic Places. *University of Pittsburgh Library System.*

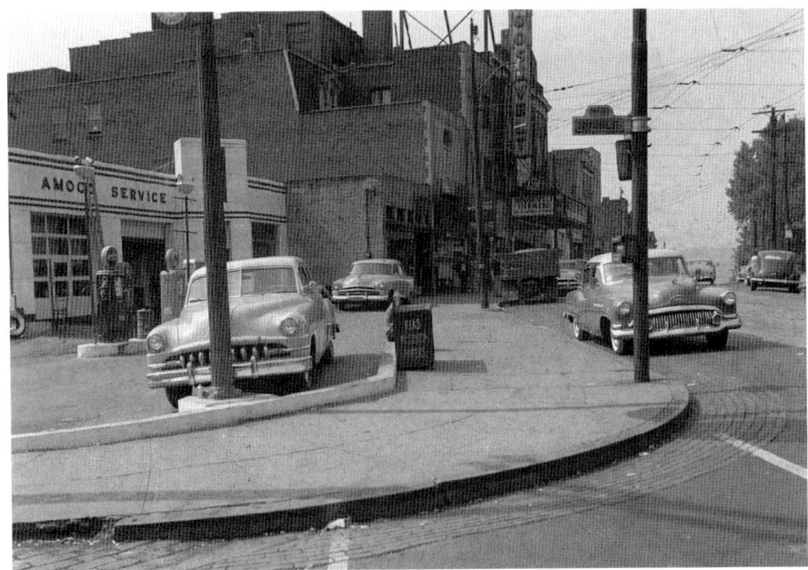

Roosevelt Theatre from Center Avenue and Dinwiddle Street. *Pittsburgh City Photographer Collection, University of Pittsburgh Digital Library System.*

Bassist and sculptor John Heard holding a bust he made of Billy Eckstine. *Courtesy of Nelson Harrison.*

Harlem Renaissance poet Claude McKay called the intersection of Wylie Avenue and Fullerton Street the "Crossroads of the World" because it was the juncture of commerce, culture and the arts in Pittsburgh's Hill District. The Hill was the intersection where the white and Black worlds came together because of the music.

Pittsburgh was a segregated town in the 1930s, '40s and '50s, but there was no segregation on the Hill. The nightspot owners challenged racial politics by ripping apart social barriers that kept the races separate. Black and tan clubs appeared on the music scene that allowed white and Black patrons to mingle, even though Black people were excluded from white-only downtown venues.

Jazz has continued to thrive in Pittsburgh despite urban renewal, which dispersed jazz to other sections of the city and suburbs. WZUM radio is dedicated to jazz music. The station's website concedes that New York, New Orleans, Chicago, Kansas City and Detroit are important jazz centers, but "Pittsburgh is right behind."

Why has Pittsburgh produced so many jazz artists? Retired judge J. Warren Watson said in an interview that many young musicians didn't want to work in the steel mills like their fathers did and spend long hours breathing in the dust and coping with heat that comes from making steel. They practiced harder at their music hoping to escape the drudgery Watson noted.

Saxophonist Art Nance joined his father working in a steel mill after he graduated from high school, but he quit after working there for a year. "Nance, you got to get out of here," he said to himself. "I hated it. I couldn't wait to get out of here," he added in an interview with the Jazz Preservation Society. Ahmad Jamal's father spent twenty-three years

Left: Kenny "Klook" Clarke on drums. Nelson's drumming style revolutionized bebop. *Courtesy of Nelson Harrison.*

Right: Drummer Joe Harris with Nelson Harrison and Ahmad Jamal at the 1994 Mellon Jazz Festival. The event is now known as the Pittsburgh International Jazz Festival and is held every summer. *Courtesy of Nelson Harrison.*

working at an open-hearth furnace. "I wouldn't have lasted there two minutes," conceded Jamal.

Dr. James Johnson Jr. recalled drummer Kenny "Klook" Clarke sitting in his living room one day talking about young aspiring Black jazz musicians wanting to avoid the life of their fathers by working in a mill. "Therefore, they put a lot more time into their craft."

Watson said all a steelworker wanted to do on weekends was leave the mill behind and dance and listen to jazz. "He got his young lady and he's holding her tight. That's all he wanted for the weekend. Monday, go back in the mill and start pouring that hot steel."

"Pittsburgh is a phenomenal place when it comes to musicians and the art form," said Ahmad Jamal in an interview recorded by the Manchester Craftsmen's Guild. "It's a rarity and still remains. Pittsburgh is not like New York. People migrate to New York. This is a town that houses people from Memphis, Kansas City, people from all over the world." Pittsburgh, he continued, has produced "a vast number of talented individuals that has very few parallels." He recorded a CD titled *Pittsburgh* and dedicated to his mother and the city.

"I still love the place. It's a special place. It's a marvelous city."

2

MUSIC CITY

When Pittsburgh was a frontier settlement in the 1760s, a musician known only by the name of "Crowder" entertained patrons with his fiddle in taverns around Fort Pitt. He played Scottish and Irish jigs, reels and minuets at watering holes with the names like McCullough's Black Boar Tavern, Mr. Morrow's Tavern and William Irwin's Inn.

Pittsburgh wasn't much of a settlement. It was inhabited by soldiers, traders, trappers and settlers heading west. Dogs, hogs and children roamed the muddy streets. There were 146 houses, 36 "huts," 6 stores and several large ponds at the Point where and the Allegheny and Monongahela Rivers merge to create the Ohio. The inhabitants were a rough, dirty lot but they loved to dance and sing. Fiddlers like Crowder provided what little entertainment there was for the hardworking and hard-drinking settlers who frequented taverns guzzling Monongahela rye and bottles of porter according to *The Planting of Civilization in Western Pennsylvania*, by Solon and Elizabeth Buck. At one wedding, a band of fiddlers entertained guests who danced ninety-two jigs, fifty-two country dances and forty-five minuets, which amounted to seven hours of dancing, according to a *History of Pittsburgh Music* by Dr. Edward G. Bayhnam.

Crowder was considered by the inhabitants of Pittsburgh as the most "important personage in town," Bayhnam wrote. "There was Crowder with fiddle and votaries making the dust fly with four-handed or rather a four-footed Irish reels, on Grant's Hill, which now is Grant Street in the heart of Pittsburgh's business district, wrote Peter Gilmore in "Traditional Music and

Ulster Culture on the Pennsylvania Frontier" in *Western Pennsylvania History*. Crowder also entertained guests at a ball in honor of Revolutionary War hero General Henry "Light Horse Harry" Lee III, the father of Civil War general Robert E. Lee.

Taverns were waystations for weary travelers and places where locals celebrated events like the Fourth of July with elaborate dinners of lamb, pork, venison and bear meat, oysters and ice cream followed by toast after toast of copious amounts of alcohol and music, according to the Bucks. Social life in frontier Pittsburgh was limited. Calvinist preachers stormed against entertainment except for church hymns. Amusement for families was restricted to barn raisings and sewing circles. Single men drank and sang in taverns, according to *Eighteenth-Century Inns and Taverns*.

Pittsburgh's music culture was born on the frontier and evolved over the centuries from spirituals and hymns to classical music, Dixieland, jazz, swing, bebop, jazz, rock 'n' roll and hip-hop. Early songs played in Pittsburgh were mainly psalms until the Scots, Irish, Germans, Welsh, English and other classically trained European musicians brought their music and folk tunes with them to America from the old world. Singing was an important part of the culture. A notice in the *Pittsburgh Weekly Gazette* in 1786 advertised for a voice teacher. "Wanted: a man who understands vocal music and can teach it with propriety; such a person will meet with good encouragement from the inhabitants of Pittsburgh."

In 1789, Edward Tyler began teaching sacred music at, of all places, McCullough's Black Boar Tavern. In 1791, the first piano arrived in Pittsburgh by pack train from Philadelphia for General Richard Butler. Pianos were considered a symbol of culture along the frontier. A decade later, Peter DeClary, who called himself the "music master of Pittsburgh," founded the Pittsburgh Music Society. DeClary began teaching piano, violin and flute. "His terms are moderate and from his long experience as a teacher, he flatters himself he will give satisfaction to those who may honor him with their instruction," read an ad in 1808 in the *Pittsburgh Weekly Gazette*.

Musical societies were beginning to form in 1805, with the Harmony Society followed by the Appolonia Society (1807), the Pittsburgh Music Society (1817), the Pittsburgh Philharmonic Society (1853), the Mozart Club (1878) and a symphony orchestra (1896). Songwriters began publishing their tunes. Dennis Loughrey, a blind poet, composed the first tune in Pittsburgh, "New Song," and it sold for six cents.

William Evans opened the first music school in 1810 and then spent the next fifty years traveling throughout western Pennsylvania teaching music and founding church choirs. William C. Peters performed the first symphony in America, *Symphony in D*, with the Harmony Society and staged a performance of Handel's "Hallelujah" chorus. Peters and John Mellor opened the first music store in 1831, selling instruments and sheet music.

The "father of American music," Stephen Foster, was born in 1826 in what is now the Lawrenceville neighborhood of Pittsburgh. The composer of "Camptown Races," "Jeanie With the Light Brown Hair" and "Beautiful Dreamer" left his mark on early American music. The Pittsburgh Theater opened in 1833, and one of its regular performers was Thomas Dartmouth Rice, an entertainer who appeared in blackface and later became the despised face of Jim Crow in the South. Five years later, *The Barber of Seville* was staged by Frances C. Wemyss. To promote the opera, Wemyss promised the public "a Dramatic Company not surpassed by any in the union," according to an advertisement in the *Daily Pittsburgh Gazette*. The old Allegheny County Courthouse on Market Square was used as the first concert hall in Pittsburgh in 1799.

Henry Kleber, a German conductor, composer and organist, created the Citizens Band, the first musical group west of the Alleghenies in 1839. He would be part of Pittsburgh's musical world for sixty-five years, according to Bayhnam's history of music. Stephen Foster was likely one of Kleber's students, as they collaborated in the 1850s, Baynham contends. Kleber opened a music store, Sign of the Golden Harp, in 1846. He was so sensitive to criticism about his music that he once was arrested for flogging a critic.

By 1840, there was a boom in theater construction, and twenty-five concert stages—along with several concert halls—opened in Pittsburgh. Foster's *Oh! Susanna* was performed by Kneass Opera Troupe at the Eagle Ice Cream Theater in 1847. The Eagle Ice Cream Theater was one of several venues where people could listen to music. There also was Foster's Gaities, Trimble's Variety, Vierhaller's Concert Garden, Sefton's Opera House and the Academy of Music, according to Lynne Conner's *Pittsburgh in Stages: Two Hundred Years of Theater.*

It was jazz, however, that put Pittsburgh on the musical map. The golden years of jazz in Pittsburgh ran from the 1920s through the 1950s, when the music was played every night at clubs in the Hill District, East Liberty, Shadyside and the North Side. "That period of time will never come again," said Chuck Austin, founder of the African American Jazz Preservation Society.

Back in the day, we really believed that if given an equal chance in training and education, encouragement and opportunity, we'd put Pittsburgh on the jazz musical map with Kansas City, Chicago or even New York. Hell, we had just as much talent.…Besides, a lot of our talent went to New York to get the recognition they could not even get here in Pittsburgh.

3

THE KING OF RIVERBOAT JAZZ

Wilma Dobie hated the frigid, snow-encrusted Pittsburgh winters and longed to hear the booming sound of a calliope from the steamboat *St. Paul* echoing off the waters of the Ohio River, which meant that spring and Fate Marable had arrived. Marable was known as the "King of Riverboat Jazz" for his annual riverboat excursions up and down the Ohio and Mississippi Rivers traveling as far north as St. Paul, Minnesota, and as far east as Pittsburgh.

Marable was a pied piper drawing people to the banks of the Ohio River with the sounds of the calliope, which was a beast to play. It produced eighty pounds of steam pressure, forcing Marable to wear gloves so the hot copper keys wouldn't burn his fingers. If you were aboard the vessel, the calliope's sound was loud enough to burst an eardrum, but on the distant shore it sounded like a siren call to people who were eager to board the *St. Paul* for a night of music and dancing on the river.

Marable would sit at the keyboard, his ears stuffed with cotton, and wearing raincoat and hat to keep the moisture from the steam from soaking his clothes. Water dripped from Marable's face onto his hands as his fingers moved quickly across the keys, morphing from one tune into another without a pause. Then, Marable stood, removed his raincoat and hat, donned a tuxedo and went to a lower deck to play for people coming aboard.

"He had the calliope on top of the boat while he used to play alone," recalled Baby Dodds in a 1994 article in a jazz magazine, the *Mississippi Rag*. "The deck down where the band played, he had little electric chimes which worked just like a calliope. He played nasty piano with the band but he would use the chimes to make the band sound a little different at times."

Marable is credited by some music historians with introducing jazz to Pittsburgh and other cities. "Fate Marable carried jazz up the Mississippi and Ohio to every town along the banks," wrote the authors of the *History of the Negro in Pittsburgh*, published by the Works Progress Administration during the Great Depression. "He himself played it. He picked up one man after another, trained him soundly in musical techniques and watched him leave the river to carry the gospel into cities inland, on the lake shore, prairies, mountainsides from coast to coast."

Jazz musician and historian Ted Gioia believes too much credit has been given to riverboats for spreading the music. Writing in the *City Journal* in 2016, Gioia credits railroads for spreading the music to places like Pittsburgh. Trains carrying southern migrants north, along with Pullman porters, help spread the music to other parts of the nation in the late nineteenth and early twentieth centuries. Nelson Harrison, a longtime Pittsburgh jazz musician, said Marable had little effect on the music. "When he ran into Mary Lou (Williams) and 'Fatha' Hines, the level of music was so high he said this is where I want to be," said Harrison in an interview.

Wilma Dobie, who lived outside of Pittsburgh in the steel town of Duquesne, was just thirteen when she first saw Marable and fell in love with the music. Their meeting was the start of a lifelong friendship that ended with Marable's death in 1947. Dobie's Sunday school teacher mom dragged her to a church picnic held on the paddle-wheeler *St. Paul*. Dobie explored the boat until she came to the deck where Marable was playing the calliope.

Dobie watched as Marable removed the cotton stuffing from his ears and put them in his coat pocket. Dobie then followed Marable to a lower deck where his band members respectfully stood waiting for him to begin the concert. "I never moved from the bandstand all afternoon," she recalled in a 1971 edition of *Storyville* magazine. Her recollections and other records are contained in the Wilma Dobie Papers at the Institute of Jazz Studies at Rutgers University.

Marable was employed by the Streckfus Steamer Company, whose excursion boats provided music and dancing at river towns from Louisiana to Missouri, to Iowa, Wisconsin, Minnesota and Cairo, Illinois, before heading east for the 981-mile trip along the Ohio River to Pittsburgh. Folks would be greeted by the mastery of Marable at the calliope and flock to the riverbanks, waiting for a chance to gaze at the twinkling lights hanging from

Fate Marable Jr. was the son of Fate Marable. The family remained in Pittsburgh. *Courtesy of Nelson Harrison.*

the steamship's three decks before boarding the boat as it churned a foamy cascade in the water.

Dobie was a lifelong jazz fan. She graduated from the University of Pittsburgh and worked in public relations, promoting the careers of singer Maxine Sullivan and pianist Earl Hines, who were both from Pittsburgh. She was a jazz enthusiast and became a journalist and jazz critic as well as Marable's confidant.

At one time, Marable's floating orchestra was considered the best dance band in the nation, with Johnny St. Cyr on banjo, George "Pops" Foster on drums, Baby Ridgely on trombone, Baby Dodds on drums, Davey Jones on mellophone, Paul Dominguez on violin, Sam Dutry on clarinet, Norman Mason on trumpet and a young coronet player named Louis Armstrong.

When he was performing in Pittsburgh, Marable hired a teenage Earl Hines to play piano. Hines would sneak out of his home in the evening with a pair of long pants hidden beneath his clothes so he could wear them when he performed in Marable's band when the *St. Paul* was docked in Pittsburgh. Nelson Harrison said in an interview that Marable's son Fate Marable Jr. once told him that so many passengers on the steamboat moved to the side of the boat where Hines was playing that the vessel began to list because of the weight displacement.

Jazz arrived in Pittsburgh as the nation's social mores were changing. Women's skirts had risen to the knee by 1924. Words like *sheik* and *flapper* were introduced into the lexicon. The city's clergy, especially Black ministers, didn't like jazz or the changes it brought. They blamed jazz for a decline in church attendance and a lessening of morals. White Pittsburgh initially embraced jazz because the Black clergy and intellectuals viewed it as a reminder of southern oppression. "Most Negro intellectuals still regard jazz as a product and symbol of the ghetto and mistook it for a minstrel show without make-up," wrote writer and critic Nat Hentoff in the *Commonweal* magazine in 1961.

Marable was captivated by the new sound of jazz coming out of New Orleans. "We were going in and out of New Orleans all the time and I began to notice the type of music playing there. It just got under my skin," he said. Marable was born December 2, 1890, in Paducah, Kentucky. His mother, Elizabeth Wharton Marable, was known as "Lizzie." She was a former slave and piano teacher who refused to let her son near the instrument, but Marable kept toying with the keys, so his mother relented and taught him to read and play music.

By two he had performed his first piece, "Anna Laurie." He was one of eleven graduates in his high school class in Paducah, and newspapers noted the demand for him to play at school events. Captain John Streckfus heard of Marable's reputation as a musician and found him shining shoes in a Paducah barbershop. He offered Marable a job in 1907, which was the beginning of a long relationship with the Streckfus family.

Streckfus started his steamboat business hauling cotton north and coal south, but faster steam-operated railroad engines threatened to bankrupt his company at the turn of the twentieth century, so he embarked on a new venture. He refitted his vessels in 1901 with large dance floors and began hiring musicians to lead orchestras for river excursions. His first bandleader was Charlie Mills, who was hired in 1903. Marable replaced Mills four years later. Streckfus also wanted his travelers to do more than just sit and enjoy the scenery as they floated downriver, so he installed a calliope on his steamships and ordered Marable to play music specified by Streckfus, who was also a musician.

Streckfus knew exactly what songs he wanted his bands to play. He attended band rehearsals and kept time with a stopwatch. He demanded the musicians play sixty beats a minute for foxtrots and ninety beats for one-step dances. He wanted his orchestras to appeal to the very best class of people and only wanted songs performed that reflected his musical tastes.

"Captain Joe Streckfus was very particular about music on the Streckfus excursion boats," recalled a musician. "He would attend rehearsals, tap his feet with his watch in his hand, and if the band failed to keep the proper tempo somebody got hell. If it happened too often, there were new faces on the bandstand."

Marable was a slender man with a receding hairline who had long arms and hands that he draped with expensive suits. He always had a cigar clenched in his mouth, according a description in the *WPA History of the Negro in Pittsburgh*. He talked so rapidly that his words ran together without a breath in between. Marable sported a moustache and wore his hats tilted at jaunty angle to give him a rakish look.

His musical influence helped develop what is known as the "Pittsburgh sound," a mixture of urban swing and blues. The Pittsburgh sound has been difficult to define, and some musicians are at a loss to define it. Drummer Roger Humphries, in a recorded interview at the Manchester Craftsmen's Guild, said the music is best defined by people outside of Pittsburgh. "Whatever it is, it must be good because everybody likes it." Some musicians find it hard to define the sound while others believe it is a mixture of blues and swing. Others claim it is "an attitude toward playing that is difficult to express in words," writes Kenan F. Foley in his doctoral dissertation at the University of Pittsburgh, "The Interpretation of Experience. A Contextual Study of the Art of Three Pittsburgh Drummers."

Pete Henderson, a trumpet player, compared the sound to a dialect. "There's a dialect....You'd have to live here to hear the dialect," he said in an interview with the African American Jazz Preservation Society. "There's a swing. We have a lot to do with that East Coast Swing. We got a Pittsburgh rhythm. You hear cats play, it's swing."

Marable also is credited as the founder of the school of Pittsburgh jazz piano, influencing Pittsburgh pianists Mary Lou Williams, Earl "Fatha" Hines, Erroll Garner, Billy Strayhorn, Ahmad Jamal, Dodo Marmarosa and Johnny Costa.

Pete Henderson jamming at the Hill House in the Hill District. *Courtesy of Nelson Harrison.*

Marable was seventeen when he went to work for Streckfus, who paired him with violinist Emil Flindt on the initial voyages. "That's all we had. Each year we added one more piece until we had what we thought was a great big band four pieces—piano, violin, trumpet and drums. All of them white boys but we played strictly ragtime," Marable recalled in an article contained among the papers of Wilma Dobie at the Institute of Jazz Studies at Rutgers University.

Marable was well respected among musicians and the populace who turned out to hear his music. Ads in the *Pittsburgh Press* billed Marable as the "king of the ivories" and touted the arrival of Marable's Cotton Pickers. "Dance in the cool, refreshing breeze on the river's Gay White Way," read another ad. In cities with heavily ethnic populations, like Pittsburgh, Marable often performed at nationality days such as Hungarian and Serbian Days and other neighborhood celebrations.

In 1912, Illinois's *Rock Island Argus* wrote about an upcoming visit by Marable, noting that "when Fate allows his fingers to wonder dreamingly over the brass keys all lovers of ragtime sit up and take notice." The article called Marable a "demon calliope artist, who is generally considered to be the premier harmonic tooter of the Mississippi." In 1933, the *Missouri Herald* called him "Professor Fate Marable, the piano wizard. Fate Marable is not only a marvelous piano player, but he has the happy faculty of surrounding himself with master musicians so that his aggregation can dispense dance music that has perfect rhythm and harmony."

On a journey to Cairo, Illinois, Marable was leading a rendition of "Turkey in the Straw" on a steamboat that was part of an armada of vessels carrying President Theodore Roosevelt. When Roosevelt heard Marable play, the president danced a jig to Marble's music on the deck of the SS *Mississippi*.

Marble fronted several bands that played on the boats. The first year he went on the river was with the Jaz-E-Saz Orchestra that featured Louis Armstrong. That was followed by Fate Marable and his Cotton Pickers and later Fate Marable's Society Syncopators. Marable penned only one composition, "Barrel House Rag," and recorded two songs during his career: "Frankie and Johnny" and "Pianoflage."

He demanded that his musicians be musically proficient but also literate. He required them to be able to read music. Most of them played by ear, so the steamboats became a floating conservatory where Marable taught musicians to read music and other technical skills they needed to be first-class musicians. Marable hired Armstrong knowing he couldn't read music. Laurence

Bergreen's biography, *Louis Armstrong: An Extravagant Life*, offers Armstrong's account of Marable's influence. "I learned very quickly," said Armstrong.

> *Of course, I could pick out a tune fast for my ears were trained. I could spell a little too, but not enough for Fate Marable's band. Fate knew all this when he hired me. That was enough for him.... Being a grand and experienced musician, he knew that just by hanging around musicians who could read music I would automatically learn myself. Within no time I was reading everything he put in front of me.... Fate was a very serious musician. He defied anybody to play more difficult than he did. Every musician in New Orleans respected him.*

Marable spent time in after-hours clubs in the Hill District drinking and talking about music with local musicians. He would down water glasses filled with gin and chase the gin with whiskey and beer before dozing off half-asleep in a chair, according to a *WPA History of the Negro in Pittsburgh*. "He is notoriously reserved on all subjects but music, slightly touched by arrogance, used to telling people what to do."

Marable didn't brook any misbehavior among his musicians. He was a stern band leader who could be cruel at times. While he was a heavy drinker, he forbade his musicians from drinking. "He was never able to settle down until he primed himself with couple of slugs of whiskey," recalled trumpeter Clark Terry in Bergreen's biography of Armstrong. "It used to be strange. He lived close to a bar but instead of having a jug up by the bed to wake up and hurriedly, before he brushed his teeth, put on—sometimes in his pajamas, run around the bar and get a drink and then he would start his day."

Marable likely was a functioning alcoholic. "He could be a sloppy drunk but he'd hit that piano," said Leon King in a 1994 article in the *Mississippi Rag*. Heavy drinking may have led to his hospitalization in 1930. Former band mates Louis Armstrong and Zutty Singleton held a benefit to raise money for Marable, who was in a Missouri hospital. Marable was penniless and needed the money to get to New York, reported the *New York Age*.

In 1945, Marable wrote Dobie when he was in the hospital and told her that he had stopped drinking for thirty-six days "and do I feel good and HOW." "Don't even drink beer or nothing. Surprising, eh! I am ready to finish that manuscript that I started and do not need any whiskey to help me soothe my nerves. I do not expect to take another drink until Halloween.... I seem to be living in a different world."

Marable and Dobie collaborated on his autobiography, of which he hand-wrote several chapters and mailed them to Dobie. The chapters talked about the reception he received from audiences and his skill at playing the calliope. "Fate, a musician and band leader from birth, had the crowd screaming and yelling over his playing of the Grand Old Flag." In another, he wrote, "On the piano Fate was an immediate success but upstairs on the calliope he was still a 'rookie' and so green he thought if had got too much steam it might blow up."

He also recounts the dissatisfaction that Streckfus had about Marable's handling of the calliope and ordered him to keep practicing. "From that day on, Fate has asked no quarter from any caliope [*sic*] players today living and still is tops among caliope players."

Marable's heavy drinking may have caused tension between him and Dobie, and his relationship with her may have been more than platonic. judging by the tone of his letters. When they first met, Dobie was thirteen, while Marable was in middle age. The letters between them reveal Marable's deep affection for her. In one letter, he implores her to send a photograph of herself and pledged to her that he would stop drinking. "Have you a picture of yourself since you moved to New York? If you have, send me one, if you have not, get me one made and send me the bill."

He even tried to persuade her to move to St. Louis, where jobs were plentiful for "a hip chick like you." In 1942, he wrote to Dobie about his plans to come to New York to see her, adding, "I want to see the Wilma Dobie I used to know. Has your heart softened since you moved to New York? Please answer this."

Pittsburgh became home to the Marable family in 1937, although Fate later divided his time between Pittsburgh and St. Louis. "When we were kids, we traveled on the boat," said Fate Marable Jr. "We lived in St. Louis, we lived in New Orleans. We moved around quite a bit," he told author Gene Ferritt in 1967 for his book *Swing Out: Great Negro Jazz Bands.* Marable's wife, Isadora, died in Pittsburgh in 1996, followed by Fate Marable Jr. in 2005— another son, William, died in 1984—and his daughter, Isadora Sandidge, in 2015.

Marable spent the remaining years of his life playing the piano at the elegant Victorian Club in St. Louis starting in 1942. "I enjoy this kind of work, for you don't have all the worries you have with a band," Marable wrote to Dobie in the summer of 1945. "But I think I will reorganize a band after the war is over. What do you think?"

He reminisced about his days on the river in an interview with a reporter for the *St. Louis Globe-Democrat* in 1940. "No singing, no dancing, just me at the piano playing requests of the patrons and the things I desire to play," he wrote. "I miss those days sometimes but 1907 is a long way from 1940, and I think I've added ten years to my life by giving up the worry of taking care of an orchestra. We sure had fun though."

The letters between Marable to Dobie became shorter and the intervals longer. Marable had mailed Dobie handwritten chapters of his autobiography while she was working in Paris. Then they stopped arriving. Dobie sensed Marable was ill. Fate Marable died in St. Louis in 1947. He was fifty-six. He is buried in the Oak Grove Cemetery in Paducah, and his small headstone has an etching of a piano with musical notes flowing across the granite. His epitaph reads, "Musician and director from 1906 to 1940 on the Streckfus Steamboats plying the Mississippi River during the era of Dixieland Jazz."

His passing was largely ignored by the media. He rated a paragraph in the *Pittsburgh Post-Gazette*; it noted his death and referred to him as the "king of riverboat jazz." The *Pittsburgh Courier* published only a bit more information on Marable's death. The *New York Times* devoted only two paragraphs.

It's unclear whether Dobie was serious about ghostwriting Marable's autobiography since there are no surviving letters from her to Marable. Nevertheless, she expressed sadness over the death of a man who was an important figure in the world of riverboat jazz. "We never did write that book," said Dobie.

times is gittin ha'd
money gittin might scare
soons I sell my cot'n
I'se going to leave this place

4

BOUND FOR THE PROMISED LAND

African musical traditions survived the arduous and dangerous trips from the cotton fields, gin mills and honky-tonks of the South to cities like Pittsburgh, where they were embraced by Black and white alike, wrote jazz pianist Billy Taylor in his 1975 doctoral dissertation, "The History and Development of Jazz Piano: A New Perspective for Educators." In addition to being a musician, Taylor also was an educator and broadcaster who tried, through his music and writing, to clarify the role African songs and chants played in the development of jazz and what made it "America's classical music."

African music shaped Dixieland, the blues and jazz by its integrating different sounds and rhythms from drums, xylophones and banjo. These traditions were passed down from one generation to the next in work and dance songs as well as religious tunes. They began with enslaved Africans, who used sound to express their feelings and aspects of everyday life.

"Music was solace. It was a community builder, and voice for hope during enslavement and afterwards in the days of Reconstruction and Jim Crow," wrote Steven Lewis in "Musical Crossroads: African American Influence in American Music," a 2016 article in *Smithsonian* magazine.

Many Pittsburgh jazz artists had family roots in the South. Pianist Mary Lou Williams was born in Atlanta, Georgia, before moving to the city with her family when she was four. Although guitarist George Benson was born in Pittsburgh's Hill District, his family's roots were in South Carolina. Bassist William "Bass" McMahon came to Pittsburgh from Birmingham,

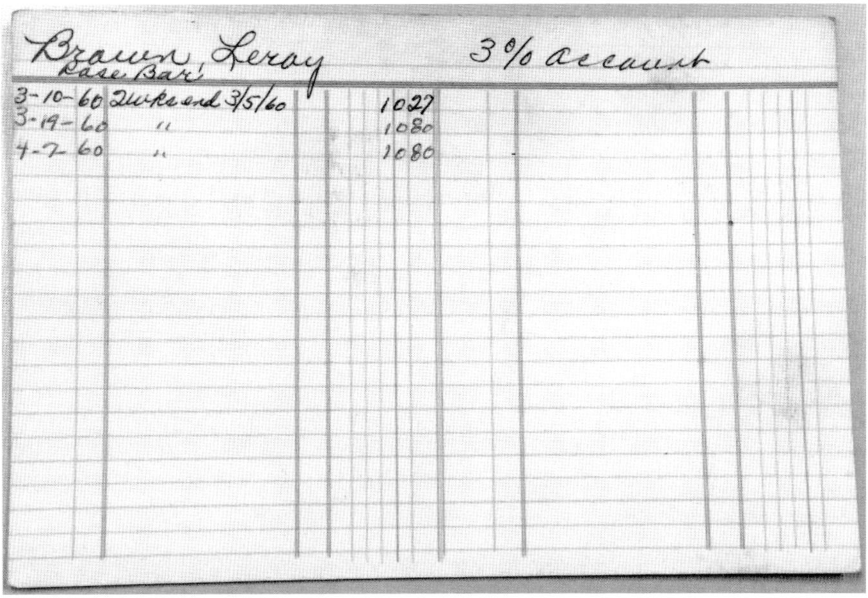

Leroy Brown union card. *African American Jazz Preservation Society of Pittsburgh Oral History Project University of Pittsburgh Library System.*

Alabama. Linton Garner, the brother of Erroll Garner, was born in Thomasville, North Carolina.

Saxophonist LeRoy Brown was born in Waycross, Georgia. Drummer Kenny "Klook" Clarke's father, Charles Spearman, also was born in Waycross, while drummer Art Blakey's family hailed from Alabama. Guitarist James "Blood" Ulmer came from South Carolina.

Trombonist Grover Mitchell, who led the Count Basie Orchestra, was born in Whatley, Alabama, but moved North. Orchestra leader George Hudson was born in Stonewall, Georgia, and was raised in Pittsburgh before establishing himself in St. Louis. Nelson Harrison, who also toured with Basie, had family roots in Alabama. Pittsburgh jazz impresario Gus Greenlee, who owned the famous Crawford Grill in the Hill District, was born the grandson of slaves in North Carolina.

These newly arrived migrants from the South injected a new energy and music into the Hill District, especially at the clubs along Wylie and Centre Avenues, filling nightspots like the Collins Inn, the Humming Bird, the Musician's Club, the Sawdust Trail, the Ritz and the Bailey Hotel. Guitarist Joe Negri said in an interview that immigrants—Black and white—were a driving force in Pittsburgh's musical evolution. "Almost every house had a

Herron and Wylie Avenues. *University of Pittsburgh Library System.*

piano in it. It was immigrant (parents) who got kids into music and move up in the world," said Negri, whose father encouraged him and his brother, Bobby Negri, a pianist, to pursue music, leading them to have successful musical careers.

Migrants flowed into Pittsburgh from southern states for a number of reasons. Pittsburgh's industries needed their labor since World War I halted immigration from central and eastern Europe. Many Black southerners were tired of living under Jim Crow, which kept them under the thumb of white people who controlled their daily lives. Failure to show proper deference, looking at a white woman the wrong way or insisting on the right to vote could get a Black person lynched.

Letters from southern Black people to northern relatives revealed the everyday violence African Americans faced if they remained in the South, according to the 1919 publication of *Letters of Negro Migrants 1916–1918*, edited by Emmett J. Scott. The letters reveal the fear and frustration that sharecroppers and others faced. One wrote:

> *We have to be shot down here like rabbits for every little orfence as I seen an orcurince hapen down this after noon when three depties from the shrief office an one negro spotter came out and found some of our raice mens in*

> *a crap game and it makes me want to leave the south worse than I ever did when such things hapen right at my door.*

Black Americans lived in a society that meant drinking from separate water fountains, having to sit in separate waiting rooms in doctors' offices and bus stations or using different telephone booths. Black people also had to stand in separate bank lines to conduct business and were forced to use separate Bibles when taking an oath in court. A poem published by the *Chicago Defender* on November 11, 1916, sums up the reasons for the mass exodus. A stanza from the poem reads:

> *Hasten on, my dark brother, duck the "Jim Crow" laws.*
>
> *No "Crackers" north to slap your mother, Or knock you in the jaw.*
> *No "Crackers" there to seduce your sister, Nor hang you to a limb,*
> *And you're not obliged to call them mister, Nor show your teeth at them.*

A notorious little bug from Mexico that feasted on cotton, known as the boll weevil, was another reason for the Black exodus. In 1915–16, the boll weevil devastated cotton crops in Louisiana, Mississippi, Alabama, Georgia and Florida, throwing the southern economy into a panic. Banks refused to extend credit to planters. The price of cotton fell. Planters reduced the number of acres they set aside for cotton and began planting other crops, which required fewer field hands, wrote Emmett J. Scott in *Negro Migration During the War.*

The bug, only a quarter of an inch long, is dependent on cotton. The weevil eats cotton fibers, lays its eggs on the buds and then hibernates. It can produce eight generations a year, according to a 2008 study, "The Impact of the Boll Weevil, 1892–1932," by Fabian Lange, Alan L. Olmistead and Paul W. Rhode.

Cotton was the cornerstone of southern agriculture. Growing cotton depended heavily on labor, but African American sharecroppers equated the agricultural practice as another name for slavery because it kept them tied to the land with few financial rewards. Erskine Caldwell's *Tenant Farmer* is a book about the plight of poor white tenant farmers and sharecroppers and the deprivation they were forced to live with. Caldwell was a struggling, little-known writer at the time he wrote the book but soared to success with his novels *Tobacco Road* and *God's Little Acre.*

Sharecroppers were dependent on land owners, and their crops were security for the money spent on food, tools, seeds and clothing. Tending the crops, especially cotton, was labor-intensive and required constant care. Cotton plants had to be thinned out, chopped, weeded and protected against the wind and rain. Everybody in the family had to be in the fields from dawn to dusk or they faced the loss of credit in the company stores, which were owned by the planters. In the fall, the cotton had to be picked quickly to prevent rain damage, ginned so impurities were removed, baled and sold. It was a crime in southern states if a sharecropper left the land before the harvest, and he could be hunted down if debts were not paid.

White landowners took advantage of Black sharecroppers by cheating them out of their fair share of the sale of cotton and by charging exorbitant fees and prices for commodities that they needed to survive, according to a U.S. Senate report on labor and capital in 1885. The courts offered little help for sharecroppers because the justice system favored the white planters.

Depending on the size of their families, sharecroppers could tend between fifteen and forty acres from a plantation owner. They also received between fifteen and fifty dollars in living expenses to survive until harvest time. Planters kept Black farmers in virtual peonage and debt by requiring they purchase seed and tools on credit that was repayable after the harvest, according to Nicholas Lemann's *The Promised Land: The Great Black Migration and How It Changed America*.

Rain meant no work, and no work meant farmers had to buy food on credit, which plunged them further into debt at the end of the growing season. Picking cotton was hard, backbreaking work. Farmers had to stoop over or crawl on their knees to pick the buds, but the stems contained thorns that bloodied a picker's hands, leaving them calloused. Once a seventy-five-pound bag was filled, it had to be lugged to the cotton gin to remove any seeds from the fibers. Cotton prices could be unpredictable. In 1919, the price of a pound of cotton dropped from a dollar a pound to ten cents a year later.

Then there was the powerful, unpredictable Mississippi River, which devastated twenty-seven thousand square miles of land, according to *Rising Tide: The Great Mississippi Flood of 1927 and How It Changed America*. The Mississippi flowed in an uneven course with unpredictable currents. Heavy rains starting in August 1926 flooded the central United States. By September, more rain had caused the Mississippi to swell, swallowing up more land.

The rains stopped in October, but by January 1, 1927, the river had reached flood stage from Cairo, Illinois, to New Orleans. Tornadoes in March in the lower Mississippi Valley sent water overflowing levees for 1,100 miles from Cairo to the Gulf of Mexico. Damage estimates ranged from $246 million to as high as $1 billion while the death toll ranged from 246 to 313. The exact number was impossible to determine because of the number of people swept away in the water or buried in the thick mud.

People huddled on rafts as water engulfed farmland. Plantation owners feared that northern labor agents would descend on the stricken South to recruit Black laborers to work in the north. Fearful southern governors mobilized the National Guard in their states to house Black farmers in segregated relief camps to force them to work. White authorities forced Black sharecroppers to help rebuild the levees and fill sandbags. "Segregation, lynching, economic exploitation and the denial of educational freedom, justice and constitutional rights had filled Negro's cup of bitterness to overflowing," wrote Abraham Epstein in his 1926 study *The Negro Migrant in Pittsburgh*.

Between 1870 and 1910, an estimated 470,000 African Americans fled the South for the North, Midwest and West. In the next decade, another 450,000 made the trek north. Between 1916 and 1940, an estimated 1.6 million Black people fled the south depleting the region's main source of labor. More than 300,000 migrants settled in the Hill District of Pittsburgh and in the surrounding mill towns of Homestead, Braddock, Duquesne, Rankin and McKeesport, finding jobs in the steel mills, coal mines and manufacturing plants in Pittsburgh. The lure of better wages in the North was another factor. Farm workers in the South earned an average of seventy-five cents a day while factory workers in the North earned as much as four dollars a day, according to the *Crisis*, the official magazine of the NAACP.

This second wave of migration saw five million more Black southerners arrive, increasing the Black populations of Pittsburgh, New York, Chicago, Philadelphia, Cleveland and Detroit, according to Professor Joe Trotter in "Reflections on the Great Migration to Western Pennsylvania," in *Western Pennsylvania History* magazine.

Escaping the South was a long and dangerous journey that could take months or years before migrants could reach their destination. They could travel by train if they could afford the price of a ticket or they might hop a freight train or hitch a ride or walk. It was expensive for migrants to head North by train because tickets ranged from fifteen to twenty dollars. Families sold family heirlooms, horses, cows and mules for far less than they paid to raise the cash for a ticket. Many started their journey without shoes or were ill, but the idea of escaping the South was contagious and spread like a disease, wrote Emmett J. Scott in his 1920 book, *Negro Migration During the*

War. Some women dressed as men to disguise their identity so they wouldn't be recognized by ticket agents or white planters.

Railroad station agents refused to sell tickets to Black people, so the migrants had to either obtain train tickets from friends or by walking to a distant station where no one knew them. If police found a Black person with a train ticket, the ticket would be confiscated. If three or more Black men were seen congregating near a train station, the police arrested them and charged them with conspiring to go north, according to Peter Gottlieb in his book, *Making Their Own Way: South Black Migration to Pittsburgh, 1916–30*, a collection of interviews of southerners who had settled in Pittsburgh.

Zonia Wilson, as the family story goes, walked the 443 miles from Spear, North Carolina, to Pittsburgh to escape the Jim Crow South during the Great Migration. She brought along her daughter, Daisy, who raised six children in a two-story cold-water flat behind a grocery store on Bedford Avenue in Pittsburgh's Hill District.

One of Zonia Wilson's grandchildren, Frederick Kittel Jr., became the Pulitzer Prize–winning playwright August Wilson, whose plays capture the life, language and hopes of the people who populated Pittsburgh's oldest neighborhood. Wilson's Pittsburgh cycle of nine plays contain places and characters of the Hill District. Zonia lived on Bedford Avenue, and her name is used in *Joe Turner's Come and Gone.* Wilson used the experience of the Great Migration as the context for his play *The Piano Lesson*, which was awarded a Pulitzer Prize for drama.

One sharecropper from South Carolina, fed up with the servitude he was forced to live in, told Gottlieb that he abandoned his cotton crop and left on a Pittsburgh-bound train in 1924. He was met by a labor agent who directed him to a steel mill in Homestead for job. "Well, as long as I stay here, I'm not going to get nowhere," the man said. "And I tied that mule to a tree and caught a train."

Southern planters feared the labor shortage caused by the exodus would cripple the economy. Some northbound trains were not allowed to stop to pick up waiting Black passengers, according to Isabel Wilkerson's *The Warmth of Other Suns: The Epic Story of American's Great Migration.*

Hundreds of southern Black citizens rode north in Jim Crow cars, forced to sit in railroad coaches located directly behind the engines, inhaling the noxious fumes from the steam engine. Others were forced to travel in baggage cars with low-class white passengers who gambled and drank their way North. These migrants packed food for the trip in baskets and old shoeboxes filled with fried chicken, biscuits, deviled eggs, cake and potato salad.

Trains from Alabama and Mississippi traveled north to Tennessee, Kentucky and Ohio before heading east toward Pittsburgh, according to the Schomburg Center for Research in Black Culture in New York. Other routes took migrants by train from Florida through Georgia, the Carolinas, Virginia and Maryland before reaching Pittsburgh and Cleveland. In the Deep South, trains traveled all the way to Wisconsin, according to a documentary, *In Motion: The African-American Migration Experience*, produced by the Schomburg Center.

As many as one hundred migrants at a time clogged the waiting rooms of southern train stations. Once they boarded the train, they began singing and stomping their feet. "I gwine to the promised land," said one man, according to individual accounts in *Negro Migration During the War.* As the trains rolled north, the faces of these migrants grew quiet, displaying their anxiety, noted a reporter for the *Pittsburgh Courier* who traveled with them on their journey. The passengers were silent, he wrote. They were leaving their families, their friends, their homes and their way of life for a new, uncertain future in a big city. They fled the South carrying bulging suitcases of various colors and size for the northward journey from the cotton fields in the Mississippi Delta, Alabama and Georgia.

In 1923, the *Pittsburgh Press* took notice of the migration that had been underway since the early twentieth century. "Day by day in every way the negro migration wave is getting larger and larger," noted the *Press*. When the train carrying the migrants passed the Mason-Dixon line it was if they had entered another world," noted a reporter. The migrants, he wrote, were motivated to leave their homeland because they had "a longing to live in a land where lynching is not a favorite pastime."

There were more than 4,700 lynchings of African Americans between 1881 and 1968. No one was hanged in Pittsburgh, but in 1920, four Black men were saved from a lynch mob by police when they were nearly hanged from a telegraph pole, according to an account in the *Pittsburgh Post*. Southern newspapers were complicit in the murders. In 1921, a mob in Arkansas hanged and set afire a sharecropper, and the newspaper advertised the killing in advance to give editors enough time to prepare special editions for the murder of Henry Lowery before a mob of five hundred jeering southerners in Nodena, Arkansas, according to the *New York Times*. Lowery had killed a white landowner and the man's daughter in a dispute over wages. The headline in the *Memphis Press*, "Kill Negro by Inches," gave a detailed account of the man's torture and slow, barbaric death.

Southern newspapers published grotesque photographs of Black men hanging from trees while crowds of white faces stood by smiling and laughing at the "strange fruit" hanging from trees. Billie Holiday recorded the song "Strange Fruit" in 1939 as a metaphor for the bodies of lynch law victims as fruit hanging from a tree. The song evoked the smell of burning flesh mixed with the smell of magnolias.

The motivation to leave the South was also fueled by stories from northern relatives who returned to the South for visits while sporting new clothes, new cars and cash to impress their families. Railroad porters and dining car waiters carried the Black-owned *Pittsburgh Courier* containing stories of Pittsburgh's cultural and social life, which attracted southern readers and prompted southern police chiefs and county sheriffs to confiscate copies of the *Courier*. The Pittsburgh Urban League distributed flyers throughout the South touting the opportunities in the North, which aided the desire to leave the South.

Labor agents working for steel companies and the Pennsylvania Railroad were stationed in southern states and recruited Black employees. The Carnegie Steel Company placed representatives in Richmond and Charlottesville, Virginia, looking for laborers. One migrant recounted how he walked past a Westinghouse plant in Pittsburgh and a company employee stopped him, asking if he needed a job. Another migrant recalled to historian Peter Gottlieb how he received a free train ticket from Jones and Laughlin officials who immediately seized his suitcase so he wouldn't quit after if he found the work too hard.

Southern white forces tried to stem the migrant tide but were unsuccessful. They argued Black people needed the South as much as the South needed them. Planters and other landowners wanted to prevent the decline of the southern economy, which depended heavily on Black workers to tend the cotton, corn and tobacco fields and to labor in the lumberyards and cotton mills.

In 1910, some 90 percent of the nation's Black residents lived in the south; by 1930, it was down to 79 percent. The Black population in America's largest cities expanded dramatically, according Harvard historian Henry Louis Gates Jr. in *Stony the Road: Reconstruction, White Supremacy, and the Rise of Jim Crow*. By 1900, the Black population of Pittsburgh increased from six thousand in 1890 to twenty-six thousand by 1900.

Newly arrived migrants faced two immediate tasks once they reached Pittsburgh. First, they had to find a place to live. Second, they needed a job. Finding a place to live was the hardest part. Many of the homes in the Hill District and other neighborhoods were unfit, according to Abraham Epstein's *Study of the Negro in Pittsburgh*. The structures were dilapidated. Wallpaper fell off, exposing bare lath. Windows were broken, ceilings and walls were damp and rooms were stuffy and unsanitary.

Migrants used old-fashioned networking to find living quarters, wrote Peter Gottlieb. "Friends, neighbors, work mates, and fellow church or lodge members from the South helped each other get to the North the same way relatives did, passing along information about Pittsburgh and offering temporary living quarters in the city to arriving friends and associates."

Many migrants found Pittsburgh disappointing. They discovered Jim Crow existed there, too. After World War I ended, racial hostility grew as returning veterans competed with Black residents for jobs that had once been theirs. Schools were segregated, and "whites only" signs began appearing in northern cities, according to *Sweet Land of Liberty: The Forgotten Struggle for Civil Rights in the North* by Thomas J. Sugrue. Racial tension increased after World War II. Some white families fled Pittsburgh to live in newly developed suburbs while Black families were not welcome in predominately white neighborhoods or had trouble obtaining mortgages from white-run banks to buy a home.

Black people were segregated. Racism was rife. Life in the Hill District was more complex than in the South. Migrants had to cope with overcrowding, poor housing and poor sanitation. The lack of space and living conditions made the Hill an incubator for tuberculosis, pneumonia, diphtheria and scarlet fever. The death rate for pneumonia was 24 percent, while TB claimed 35 percent of the residents.

A migrant farmer from Georgia arrived in Pittsburgh in 1917 with his wife and eight children. He found a job that paid $3.60 for a twelve-hour day. Two of his children died of pneumonia after living in a house with small, damp rooms that had no heat—except from a stove—and no water except what they could retrieve from a street pump.

C.E. Broadus was a tap dancer who was born in Virginia and experienced racism after moving to Pittsburgh as a child. He became a member of the *Kandy Kids*, a program featuring musically talented children on WWSW radio. The show originally was on KDKA until an announcer told the listening audience they were about to hear a group of talented "pickaninnies." Broadus also remembered having to sit in the balcony of theaters, known as "nigger heaven," whenever he went to see a movie.

A Black person walking through a white neighborhood was eyed suspiciously. Broadus once traveled to Etna just outside the city to participate in a talent contest, but the ticket taker at the theater wouldn't let him inside—even though Broadus was a contestant. White people called him racial epithets. The ticket taker called the manager, and Broadus explained why he was there and how he was being treated. To his credit, the manager told

Alvin Theater on Federal Street at Penn Avenue. The Alvin was built in 1891 and was among three iconic landmarks in the city along with the Nixon and Pitt Theaters. *University of Pittsburgh Library System.*

the white audience that if he heard one racial name called out during the performance, he would immediately close the theater.

Broadus won the talent show, earning a thirty-five-dollar-prize, but the incident left him bitter. "From that day, I've never been to Etna since," he recalled in a recorded interview with Carnegie Library's music department.

Being Black in Pittsburgh meant living in a world that was similar to the South. Pittsburgh had twenty-eight hospitals but rarely admitted a Black patient, and Black physicians were not allowed to admit a Black patient. When someone was sick, they had to rely on home remedies, patent medicines or quacks for a cure, according to *Robert L. Vann of the Pittsburgh Courier: Politics and Black Journalism*, a biography of the late publisher by Andrew Buni.

Pittsburgh has been a racially segregated city for decades, according to a 2015 study by the Urban Institute. The city has "a long history of segregation and racial prejudice," the study reported. Schools, amusement parks and housing in white neighborhoods were off-limits to Black residents.

Even big-name stars could not escape Jim Crow. Count Basie, Duke Ellington, Cab Calloway and Lionel Hampton could not stay in white-only hotels when they performed in Pittsburgh. Instead, they had to find lodging in Hill District listed in the Green Book, a directory of Black-owned businesses that catered to Black clientele.

Whenever Duke Ellington came to Pittsburgh, he rode in his own Pullman car and stayed there during his engagement. Musicians often found lodging at the Avenue Hotel, the Elmore, the Flamingo and the Ellis, all located in the Hill, according to "Just Passing Through: A Haphazard History of Pittsburgh Hotels" in the online magazine *Glassblock*.

White people would not shake hands with Black people or address them as "Mr." or "Mrs." according to historian David E. Kyvig in *Daily Life in the United States 1920–1940: How Americans Lived Through the Roaring Twenties and the Great Depression*.

Isaly's, a chain of ice cream parlors known for its chipped chopped ham and Klondike ice cream bars, would not allow Black patrons to eat inside their stores. They could buy one of Islay's towering whitehouse cherry ice cream cones at the counter but had to eat it outside. While white diners were served on china, Black customers had to make do with eating off paper plates. Waiters poured salt into the coffee and soup of Black customers at restaurants where they were not welcome. Black students were called racially offensive names. The Atlantic & Pacific Tea Company placed a storefront ad in stores depicting a "Mammy."

Swimming pools were segregated. A public pool in the Highland Park neighborhood of Pittsburgh was for white swimmers only. In 1950, when a group of Black bathers tried to integrate the pool, they were attacked with bricks and rocks. Kennywood, an amusement park located outside of the city, allowed Black churches to hold picnics at the park but refused to allow them to swim there. In South Park, Allegheny County built two pools, one for white patrons and the other exclusively for Black use. African Americans had to sit in the balcony if they wanted to watch a movie or attend a band concert. Radio stations routinely referred to Black performers as "dusky," "darkies," "coons" and "pickaninnies." The city's major department stores—Kaufmann's, Gimbels, Horne's, Rosenbaum's and Frank & Seder's—refused to hire Black salespeople. Some industries had separate bathrooms for their Black and white workers, according to an article by Dr. Larry Glasco in *Western Pennsylvania History Magazine*.

In 1950, the Republican Party in Pittsburgh placed election ads on billboards that were thinly disguised racism. The ads urged voters to "Vote Republican" and depicted a dark-colored hand reaching for a white child with the warning "Make Our Homes and Streets Safe."

Black workers always were hired at the lowest pay regardless if they were skilled or unskilled workers. In addition to jobs in the mines and mills, they found employment as bricklayers, mechanics, tailors, porters, janitors or chauffeurs. Most migrant workers in Pittsburgh earned between $2.00 and $3.60 a day, which allowed them to send money home. But their rents were exorbitant. In 1917, it cost an individual $21.00 a week to live in the Hill District, according to Epstein's study. Rooms were rented for $1.50 to $1.75 week.

The newly arrived migrants also faced discrimination by Pittsburgh-born Black people who considered themselves among the elite in the African American community class structure. They looked down on the southern-born migrants and their crude manners and ways. Some of this attitude carried over into the music. Upper-class Black residents—who referred to themselves as "old Pittsburghers"—didn't want to be reminded of African musical traditions or memories of slavery and oppression.

In a 1923 editorial, the *Pittsburgh Courier* urged compassion toward the new arrivals: "We can not [*sic*] expect strangers to know our customs, our habits, and various social ordinances without some instruction." Southerners complained the Pittsburgh's Black community failed to understand the hardship they faced below the Mason-Dixon line. They were not welcome in the Baptist churches in Pittsburgh and so began attending the raucous religious services of storefront churches, which were heavy on singing, dancing and music.

In the 1920s, migrants faced a resurgence of the Klan in Pittsburgh and an increase in violence. The Klan posed a threat not only to African Americans but also to Jews and Catholics. Membership in the KKK increased to one thousand by 1921, and it brazenly held public rallies in 1922 in nearby Wilkinsburg. The *Pittsburgh Post* reported that a fight between fifty Black people and thirty white resulted in the killing of one man after a group of white men raided a dance hall. Klan marches in Carnegie, just outside the city, and in Scottdale in Westmoreland County ended in violence and death in 1923.

Black families living in the Hill District complained about police brutality in 1925 after officers broke into homes without warrants and arrested people without justification, according to the *Pittsburgh Press*. When a Black man was accused of killing a white man and assaulting his daughter, vigilantes were prepared to storm the homes in Stowe Township, just across the Ohio River from Pittsburgh. The mob gave Black residents, many of whom were from the South, twenty-four hours to get out of the township. Police then allowed the vigilantes to scour the community to make sure they had left.

The Black exodus created a severe labor shortage in some states, leading white residents to try and intimidate African Americans from leaving, according to *Making Their Own Way: Southern Black Migration to Pittsburgh, 1916–1930* by Peter Gottlieb. Five Black men on a northbound train were confronted by a white man who knew where they were headed. "Yo niggahs going north, eh? We all just shippin five of yo back from thah." The men froze to death, the man said, in Pittsburgh, pointing to five coffins in the next car. That type of intimidation failed to deter many Black southerners—they kept coming.

Southern states sent commissions to northern cities offering one-way railroad tickets to migrants "who found northern opportunity an elusive mirage," encouraging them to return home. Few accepted the offer. The January 1920 issue of the *Crisis* magazine, published by the NAACP, said southerners must be dreaming if they thought the migrants would want to return.

"Time may come when the South will awaken from its dream of hordes of disillusioned negroes flocking back to their 'best friends' and will realize the gold mine of negro labor which it had lost."

5

THE HILL

Overlooking the gleaming downtown Pittsburgh skyline is the Hill District, a once thriving economic, social and cultural African American enclave that was a city within a city. The Hill was set apart from white Pittsburgh by race, income and culture, but now the neighborhood is on the brink of a renewal. After decades of broken promises, plans are underway to inject $750 million in private money into twenty-eight acres in the lower Hill District in a mix of residential and commercial development.

The Hill District helped Pittsburgh carve out a reputation as a center for jazz. Musicians and fans flocked to the nightclubs along Wylie Avenue to places like the Crawford Grill, the famed Musicians' Club, the Hurricane Lounge, the Bambola, the Loendi Club or the Roosevelt Theater. Jazz royalty frequented the clubs: Duke Ellington and Count Basie, among others, rushed to Hill District nightspots once their performances ended to listen to other artists perform. Members of touring bands would gather at the Musicians' Club to jam with musicians in wild all-night sessions in which one player tried to outdo the other with musical skill.

Since Black people were not welcome in downtown, pharmacies, a grocery store, nightclubs, restaurants, five movie theaters, a department store, professional offices and the influential black newspaper, the *Pittsburgh Courier*, were located in the Hill. The Hill was home to a professional baseball team, the Pittsburgh Crawfords, a powerhouse in the National Negro

Above: Hill District businesses. The Hill was a city within a city with its own stores, pharmacies, professional offices, nightclubs and movie theaters. Since African Americans were not welcome in white stores, clubs and theaters, they created their own community in the Hill District. *University of Pittsburgh Digital Library System.*

Left: Crawford Grill #2. *Courtesy of Nelson Harrison.*

League. Then came urban renewal and the wrecking ball in the 1950s, which destroyed the lower part of the neighborhood. Jazz clubs disappeared in a cloud of dust along with a part of the city's musical legacy.

The Hill is a long, sloping neighborhood that runs from downtown to Oakland. It is bordered by the downtown on the west, the Strip District and Polish Hill to the north, Uptown on the southwest and Oakland to the east and south. Its history dates to early Pittsburgh when William Penn's grandson owned the land; it later contained estates, farms, coal mines and a village populated by freed slaves.

The Hill served as the background for nine of playwright August Wilson's ten Pittsburgh plays. *Fences*, *The Piano Lesson*, *Joe Turner's Come and Gone*, *Two Trains Running*, *Seven Guitars*, *Jitney*, *Gem of the Ocean*, *Radio Golf* and *King Hedley II* are tributes to the Hill District, wrote Betina Jones in her 2011 doctoral dissertation, "This Is Me Right Here: August Wilson and Pittsburgh's Hill District."

At the turn of the twentieth century, the Hill had become an ethnic neighborhood inhabited by Germans, Irish and Slavs filling the squalid tenements. Jews lived on the southern end of the Hill, the Italians on the north. Syrian, Armenian, Lebanese and Greek immigrants resided on the lower end along Bedford and Webster Avenues.

Wylie Avenue was the heart of the Hill District. Its narrow streets were paved with Belgian block. The doorways of buildings were littered with trash. August Wilson, who was raised in the Hill District, wrote about the rickety porches, crumbling sidewalks, jitney stations, diners and barbershops where men congregated.

The nickname for the Hill District was "pot likker flats." Residing there meant living amid poverty, disease, crime and vice. There were saloons, gambling joints, dope dens, pawn shops, pool rooms and brothels. Some restaurants smelled so bad that the odor ruined one's appetite. The streets in the Hill District were covered with debris. The housing was dingy. Plaster walls were cracked, creating dust. Windows were broken. Rooms were damp and unsanitary. Roofs sagged, and walls leaned so precipitously that they looked like they would collapse at any moment.

Wylie Avenue in the Hill District looking east from Elmore Street. *University of Pittsburgh Digital Library System.*

Ray Sprigle, a Pulitzer Prize–winning reporter for the *Pittsburgh Post-Gazette*, wrote in 1938 how greedy slum landlords refused to fix their buildings and forced tenants to survive in rickety apartments. City inspectors ignored building codes and refused to condemn unsafe buildings. "The law just doesn't worry much about what happens on the hill," wrote Sprigle. He found sixty-five children and their parents living in a building that had three toilets and discovered nine people living in a single room. Three years later, Sprigle revisited the Hill and found little had changed. He described the Hill as "100 acres of squalor and filth of ancient wreckage that has been decaying for half a century."

In 1943, Pittsburgh city councilman George Evans found little in the Hill District that was worth saving "and so there would be no social loss if they were all destroyed," reported the *Bulletin Index*, a weekly news magazine. "The Hill was completely worn out, like an old pair of shoes that has gone the last mile."

Life was a daily struggle. During the Great Depression, people held rent parties where cheap liquor, barbecue and music from a phonograph was

Workers haul trash in the Hill District as part of an annual clean-up. Garbage and debris covered the streets and sidewalks because city officials paid little attention to the Hill District. *University of Pittsburgh Library System.*

Tenements in the Hill District were occupied by a variety of ethnic groups—Jews, Slavs, Greeks, Syrians, Lebanese, Irish and Germans—before becoming inhabited mainly by African Americans. *University of Pittsburgh Library System.*

used to generate cash. Tenants usually raked in fifteen to twenty-five dollars from these events, which was usually enough to pay their rent, according to a *History of the Negro in Pittsburgh* by the Works Progress Administration. While jazz records filled the room, visitors swayed to the songs of blues singers Wee Bea Booze and Lil Green.

The Depression was also hard on musicians because there were fewer gigs to go around. Musicians played at clubs for free because cash-strapped owners could not afford to pay them. They passed the hat among the crowd for contributions before rushing off to repeat the performance at another club. Groups of musicians congregated along Wylie Avenue hoping a club owner would drive by looking to hire a musician for the evening.

As more Black migrants flooded the Hill District, jazz clubs and cabarets opened, attracting homesick southern migrants nostalgic for a taste of southern cuisine and music. Flush with cash from jobs in the steel mills, they pumped their money into these venues, which blossomed. "Some of these places did quite well," recalled retired Allegheny County judge Warren Watson, ninety-six, who balanced both a legal career and that of a jazz musician.

Bookies roamed street corners, accepting bets on numbers. A passerby could hear the jingle of change and the clatter of adding machines coming from storefronts that were used as counting houses where big, rough-looking men stood guard. Street vendors sold chitterlings, hog jowls, bacon rinds and turnip greens while small bars served sloe gin and beer to people sitting at wooden tables.

Makeshift food stands along Wylie Avenue sold navy bean sandwiches for a nickel and a plate of chitlins for ten cents. The aroma of cooking neck bones, ham hocks, collard greens, black-eyed peas and cornbread filled the Hill District. There was always live music and hot sex in hotels that charged overnight rates, according to "Pittsburgh Jazz Records and Beyond, 1950–1985," Carlos Pena's master's thesis at the University of Pittsburgh.

On Saturday and Sunday nights, crowds began forming outside jazz clubs on the lower end of the Hill. Men wearing their Sunday best and women dressed to the nines congregated outside the Crawford Grill waiting to get inside. Young boys waited in an alley behind the Crawford Grill for a glimpse of John Coltrane when he came outside for a break.

Jazz artists became cultural heroes for young Black men, said drummer Joe Harris. "The people knew the music and who was who in those days," Harris said in an interview contained in the Maurice Levy Oral History collection at Carnegie Library. "My parents had all the records. It was a black thing because you didn't have many black heroes."

Jazz fans might head for the Hurricane Lounge, where owner Birdie Dunlap was preparing her Brazilian fried shrimp, or to the Bambola, the Musicians' Club or the Savoy Ballroom. Others might go to Marie and Lola's and dance to jazz from the jukebox beneath dim red and green lights amid the scent of cheap incense. To enter Marie and Lola's, patrons had to climb narrow steps and then walk down a long hallway before entering a room where the air was filled with cigar and cigarette smoke.

The Hill never slept said trombonist Nelson Harrison. He recalled "people cooking barbecue in their backyards at 4:00 a.m." It was a breeding ground for young jazz musicians, who rubbed elbows with famous artists while picking up advice. "It was heaven," said Harrison in an interview.

During Prohibition, speakeasies named the Black Bottom, Big Apple and Bucket of Blood served moonshine, cheap wine and homemade beer. The beer was served in large water pitchers, which served as weapons in the event a fight broke out, wrote Hosea Taylor in his autobiography, *Dirt Street*. At the Washington Club, musicians played while big-time gamblers sat around big round tables covered in white cloth.

Sometimes national artists made surprise appearances in the clubs. Taylor recalled playing one night at the Washington Club when a young man walked up to the bandstand and asked pianist Roy Hamilton if he could sit in. Hamilton stepped aside, and the man began playing. The audience began cheering wildly as the pianist played until the sun came up. It was Art Tatum, Taylor said.

After Prohibition was repealed, Hill District nightlife was no longer secret. People drank alcohol without fear of police raids, and the speakeasies transformed into legitimate nightclubs where jazz became Pittsburgh's music. At the center of the Hill's nightlife was the Crawford Grill, the Musicians' Club, the Loendi, the Washington Club, the Celebrity Club and Stanley's Lounge. Later came the Melody Bar, the Ritz, the Blue Note, the Iron City Elks, Mutt's Hutt, Little Paris, the Bambola and the Hurricane Lounge.

Harrison, who has been playing professionally since he was a teenager, said Hill District audiences and musicians could be discriminating. "If you were Black and couldn't play, they'd say, 'oh, get out of here, man. You're not speaking the language at all,'" said Harrison in an oral history for the Manchester Craftsmen's Guild.

"Imagine going to a Baptist Church and the preacher is standing up there reading the sermon as a Presbyterian. The church would be empty, right? You go into a club you want to hear some jazz but they're playing something else. I'll be the first to leave." Harrison recalled Art Blakey once saying that real jazz was a gift from God. "From the creator, to the artist, to the people. That's as high as it can get."

Saxophonist Don Aliquo Sr. said in an interview that playing jazz is like having an addiction. "What you do is to find the right note at the right time to make you feel euphoric. That doesn't happen very often."

Publicity photo of Billy Eckstine. *Erroll Garner Archive, University of Pittsburgh Library System.*

The Hill District was less than one square mile where music played twenty-four hours a day. Erroll Garner, Earl "Fatha" Hines, Lois Deppe, Kenny "Klook" Clarke, Art Blakey, Stanley Turrentine, Billy Eckstine, Mary Lou Williams and George Benson honed their talent playing in dozens of clubs along Wylie Avenue, Fullerton Street and Centre Avenue.

Singer and bandleader Billy Eckstine began his musical career working in the clubs. "I started working in a little club called Derby Dan's, and in another place, called the Harlem Bar and then in a place called Java Jungle. At the Harlem Bar I was the emcee. I produced the shows and I checked out the waitresses," said Eckstine in Betina Jones's dissertation.

The Hill had larger venues for concerts and dancing. People flocked to the Pythian Temple, the Elmore Theater, the Savoy Ballroom and the Roosevelt Theater. Promoter Sellers McKee Hall booked acts at the Pythian Temple, owned by the Black Knights of Pythias, and named a portion of it the Savoy Ballroom. Duke Ellington appeared there with Count Basie, Fletcher Henderson, Billy Eckstine, Cab Calloway, Noble Sissle, Chick Webb and Jimmie Lunceford, according to the *Pittsburgh Courier*. In January 1932, three thousand people packed the ballroom to watch Ellington crowned the "king of jazz" in a nationwide broadcast.

In 1945, another promoter, Harry Hendel, took over the temple and renamed the basement the New Savoy, where Dizzy Gillespie, Charlie Parker, Ella Fitzgerald, Dinah Washington, Miles Davis and Nat King Cole appeared. The ballroom was illuminated with a crystal dance ball, a redwood dance floor, red velvet curtains, polished mirrors and a doorman who greeted guests, according to a description in the *Pittsburgh Courier*.

Poster advertising a Count Basie concert at Penn Shady Ballroom on Herron Avenue. *Pittsburgh City Photographer Collection, University of Pittsburgh Digital Library System.*

The Crawford Grill and the Musicians' Club were two of the most iconic spots in the Hill and were must-stops for nationally known musicians who played engagements in the city. They hurried to the Hill to play sets at the grill or jam at the Musicians' Club in musical competitions against local artists called "cutting contests." The origins of the Crawford Grill were in the first decade of the twentieth century. Businessman and promoter Gus Greenlee purchased the Collins Inn, which he renamed the Paramount Inn, before it became the Crawford Grill on Christmas Eve 1933.

The first floor of the Crawford Grill contained a bar topped in glass and a piano clad in mirrors set on an elevated stage. The next floor was for dancing. The third floor housed the private Crawford Club, where Greenlee entertained personal guests. Black and white patrons crowded the grill three deep at the bar to drink daiquiris and listen to the top Black musicians of the day perform. The Greenlee-owned Paramount Inn opened on July 4, 1933, but by Christmas Eve that year, he had renamed it the Crawford Grill for its grand opening.

Greenlee was a large man who was born in a log cabin in North Carolina and arrived in Pittsburgh about 1920. He shined shoes, worked construction and in a steel mill, drove a cab and sold moonshine out of the trunk of his taxi, earning the nickname "Gasoline Gus," according to *Sandlot Seasons: Sport in Black Pittsburgh* by Rob Ruck. Greenlee's wealth from the numbers made him an important man in the Hill. He wore custom-made white suits, black shirts and white shoes. Friends called him "Big Red" because of his reddish hair and freckles.

Many musicians learned their craft in the Hill District. Nelson Harrison, a trombone player, earned a doctorate in clinical psychology, but "I got my (musical) doctorate on the streets and from the Crawford Grill," he said in an interview for this book. Saxophonist Don Aliquo Sr. said Greenlee's partner in the Crawford Grill, Joe Robinson, talked Greenlee into hiring Aliquo to play there. "There I was, fairly green in a place that had such a reputation. I was absolutely elated to play there," he said in an interview. Trumpet player Danny Conn enhanced his musical skills playing in jazz clubs. "I learned a lot at the Crawford Grill....We waited for a chance to play," said Conn in an oral history at the Carnegie Library in Pittsburgh.

Drummer Roger Humphries, still a mainstay in Pittsburgh's jazz community, was introduced to the culture of the Crawford Grill when he was twelve years old. His family sat in a booth near the bandstand, where he listened to drummers Art Blakey and Max Roach perform. "It was amazing and opened up my whole world of music," said Humphries in a recorded interview for the Manchester Craftsmen's Guild.

"We wouldn't miss a matinee" at the grill and at the Midway Lounge, Liberty Lounge, the Hi Hat or Chappees, Humphries recalled in an interview with Kenen A. Foley for Foley's doctoral dissertation at the University of Pittsburgh in 2007, "The Interpretation of Experience: A Contextual Study of the Art of Three Pittsburgh jazz drummers."

Humphries was one of ten children and started his musical career banging on the dining room table with knives and spoons. When he was still a child, a sister took him to clubs on the North Side, East Liberty and the Hill District, where he was exposed to the city's jazz culture. By the time he was five, he was sitting in with bands at the Savoy Ballroom. "Music was looked upon as a skill, an art, it was a gift that God give you," he told Foley. "It wasn't looked upon negatively."

He auditioned for admission to the Lennox School of Music and received a scholarship and was ready to leave when he realized the scholarship covered only his tuition and not his room and board. "But we just didn't have the money. I know my dad was hurt. I know he wanted it for me. I cried. I was hurt but I got past it."

The grill was a hangout for celebrities of the music, sports and political worlds. Over the years, patrons might catch a glimpse of Roberto Clemente of the Pittsburgh Pirates, Jackie Robinson of the then Brooklyn Dodgers, Hank Aaron of the then Milwaukee Braves, Monte Irvin and Henry Thompson of the New York Giants. Louis Armstrong, Earl "Fatha" Hines, Duke Ellington and Count Basie were often Greenlee's guests in his private Rumpus Room on the grill's third floor. Boxers Sugar Ray Robinson, Joe Louis and John Henry Lewis regaled patrons at the bar with stories. Pittsburgh Steeler fullback John Henry Johnson and Satchel Paige of the Pittsburgh Crawfords were regulars along with city, county and state officials.

There actually were three Crawford Grills. One operated on Wylie Avenue from 1933 until 1951, when it was destroyed by fire. In 1943, Greenlee and partner Joseph Robinson opened Crawford Grill No 2, and it remained in business until 2003. A third version opened in Pittsburgh's North Side in 1948 but was closed by 1955. Another grill opened at Station Square in 2003 on the South Side but was out of business three years later.

Another legendary club in the Hill was the Musicians' Union Club, a place where musicians jammed, practiced, socialized, competed and found jobs. Pittsburgh-born pianist Ahmad Jamal told a radio interviewer in 1995 that he regretted the "tremendous loss" of the Musicians' Club in the name of redevelopment. Jamal said that the musicians who came to the club to participate in jam sessions were among the best in the jazz world.

Trumpet player Pete Henderson recalled the time when he and Ahmad Jamal, who was then known as Fritzie Jones, left Westinghouse High School so they could go to the club to hear Billy Eckstine and his band rehearse. At the time, Eckstine's band included Art Blakey, Gene Ammons and Dexter Gordon. "I seen history," said Henderson in a Jazz Preservation Society interview in 1998. He also remembered club president Prez Jackson telling Eckstine to hide the marijuana his band members smoking. "Billy, you get rid of those reefers," Jackson ordered.

Nelson Harrison, in an interview with Colter Harper for Harper's doctoral dissertation, said the jam sessions allowed musicians to network:

> *There were guys that would come into town that would like to mix with the locals and play and we'd have jam sessions. You never knew who'd show up. I remember Jimmy McGriff came in with Rudy Johnson, who was with Ray Charles. We went up to the Loendi Club in the Hill District on Ledley Street off of Bedford and had a jam session. "Hey man, you play pretty good, give me your number." Then somebody would call you from New York, "Hey man, I heard about you." You couldn't talk your way into it. They would have to hear you.*

Joe Harris, a drummer who was part of the bebop revolution with the Dizzy Gillespie Big Band, recalled sessions at the Musicians Club in the Hill District as times when greats from visiting bands would get together with local musicians for trying to outperform each other in cutting contests. That's where Pittsburghers such as Roy Eldridge, Billy Eckstine, Mary Lou Williams, Erroll Garner, George Benson and the Turrentine brothers, Stanley and Tommy, advanced their careers, said Harris. Harris was born in Pittsburgh's North Side and later lived in Sweden, Japan and Germany before returning to Pittsburgh to teach at Pitt.

The cutting contests were musical competitions where musicians tried to outplay each other to determine who was the better artist. Sometimes they were embarrassing. Joe Negri recalled the night Stan Getz came into the club and was humiliated by a teenage Ahmad Jamal. Getz came into the club and heard Jamal playing and was impressed by his ability. Getz was a bit intoxicated when he arrived. He announced, "I'm going to play with that kid. He sounds pretty good," recalled Negri in an interview.

"He kept calling Jamal 'kid.' Getz is a little high and a little anxious. He wanted to play 'This Song Is You.' Ahmad asks Kenton 'what key to do you want it in? Put it in your key.' Jamal put it in an odd key and ran Getz through the keys. Getz blew up and put his horn in case and left the club," said Negri, who noted Jamal resented being called kid. "That just rubbed him the wrong way." Touring musicians sometimes were afraid to challenge local talent, said Hill Jordan, a sax player who warned that in Pittsburgh, "a guy might jump off a garbage truck and play you off the stage," according to an article by the Pennsylvania Historical and Museum Commission on the history of jazz in Pennsylvania. Jordan added,

> *Joe Kennedy, the great violinist, was one of the prominent figures in the jam sessions. There was the great guitarist Ray Crawford, who started out playing saxophone; he was one of the great saxophonists. Ray Brown would come back, when he wasn't on the road; he would come back and play, too. Leroy Brown, the famous Leroy Brown in Pittsburgh. Osie Taylor, a phenomenal saxophone player. Sam Johnson, the great Sam Johnson, a pianist.*

Johnson was best friends with Erroll Garner. They practiced together. Played together. Performed in some of the same places. While Garner achieved fame, Johnson remained in the shadows working as a piano tuner for Steinway in Philadelphia in 1947. Johnson had his first lesson at seven from a man who played piano at rent parties, but the man gave up on Johnson and refused to teach him any longer. Johnson was crushed according to Nelson Harrison, who was Johnson's closest friend.

"I came home and was standing at the piano crying," Johnson told Nelson. "He said my mother came in and said 'what's wrong Sammy?' He said 'I'm going to learn to play the piano if it kills me. He said the next day feeling come over him and I understood the piano." Johnson returned to Pittsburgh in 1982, but few people in the city's music world knew of his talent. Harrison took Johnson around to gigs to play, but Johnson spent his days in his third-floor apartment playing a Casio keyboard.

Johnson started out playing in a Pittsburgh quartet known as the Four Strings, said Harrison. When Johnson left the group to move to Philadelphia, he was replaced by Ahmad Jamal, who considered Johnson a better talent. One day, in 1982, Harrison was performing at a club in Pittsburgh with Horace Lee Turner when a man walked in and announced, "I heard there's some musicians here."

The man asked Harrison if he could sit in. "You want to play something? What do you want to play?" the man asked. Harrison chose "Around Midnight." Harrison was impressed by the man's playing so he asked the mysterious pianist his name. "Sam Johnson," the man replied. "I almost fainted," Harrison recalled. Johnson, he continued, had a keen sense of beauty and sound and took songs to new technical levels. He mastered the technique of contrary motion, in which one line of music rises in pitch while the other descends at the same time.

Harrison said Johnson was a humble man who regretted the different paths he and Garner took. Erroll Garner became Erroll Garner, and Johnson was a footnote in the history of Pittsburgh jazz. Harrison remembered Johnson once telling him regretfully, "Yeah man, Erroll had it all."

Johnny Oliver told the *Pittsburgh Courier* that if a musician can make a name for himself in Pittsburgh, he could make it anywhere "One thing I like about playing in Pittsburgh is that you've really got to cut it or get laughed off the stage," Dizzy Gillespie told the *Courier*. "Seems the whole audience is made up of critics."

The Musicians Club served as the headquarters of Local 471 of the American Federation of Musicians before it merged in the 1960s with Local 60. The club was originally housed in the former Collins Inn owned by Harry Collins. "You did your job and hurried to the club…so they could play," said Chuck Austin in an interview with the Jazz Preservation Society. "For me going to the club was an exhilarating experience playing in the company of musicians was inspirational and affirming. The way they dressed, the manner in which they carried themselves, the swagger and cockiness was contagious. Outside the club we didn't have a life. All we wanted to do was come and play." George Thompson, a saxophonist, tried to emulate bebop musicians, wearing goatees, thin black ties and blazers. "We even tried to stand like the beboppers when we played," he said in a society interview.

Warren Watson, ninety-six, went to the club so he could learn from others. "I'd go to the club after one a.m. People were just beginning to play," he said in an interview. "You'd hear something you liked and you'd go ask him, 'how'd you do that?' And for the most part he'd show you." Jacques "Bill" Gambrell said the musicians who jammed at the club "were marvelous, marvelous human beings. Jam sessions were master classes in jazz. I wish more people would realize the outstanding contributions of that wonderful organization"

Pianist Walt Harper, who owned several jazz clubs in Pittsburgh, said he couldn't stay away from the club when he was young. "There were 52 weeks

Erroll Garner at the piano, 1951. *Erroll Garner Archive, University of Pittsburgh Library System.*

in a year and I was there 48 weeks of them," he said in an oral history at Carnegie Library.

In those days, everybody smoked, so the third floor would be one large smoke-filled room. "I never smoked back then but the smoke would be from the ceiling three-fourths of the way down to the floor," pianist George "Duke" Spaulding said in an oral history at the library.

"The beauty is that the Musicians Club provided a casual but controlled place for musicians to practice and perfect their instruments," said Chuck Austin. "All Black musicians were welcome from beboppers, to swingers, to jazz. That is what the Musicians Club clearly was for. It was a place where we felt we belonged. The camaraderie among the musicians was powerful.

It was such a place where even white musicians would come to pick up the latest even though we couldn't come to their Musicians Club."

Drummer John Hughes remembered cutting classes in high school so he could go to the Musicians' Club. "We would sneak away from school whenever we could, hoping for a chance to see some of the greats in the club. I would sneak out of bed and go down to some of the clubs to sit in for a drunk drummer…a drunk drummer can really mess things up," Hughes said in an interview for the Carnegie Library jazz collection.

The Musicians Club also served as a music school. Musicians like Stanley Turrentine would show up at the club for the Wednesday night jam sessions and write chord changes for a particular tune in chalk on a blackboard. "You were kind of expected to know them the next week when you came back, you know. You couldn't even get on the stand if you didn't know the changes, man," said George Thompson.

Since Black jazz musicians couldn't perform at white-owned clubs because of Jim Crow traditions, they played a circuit of Black clubs on the Hill and in East Liberty and Homewood known as the "chitlin circuit." "It was our renewal, our sense of self confidence and self-worth after discriminatory treatment all day in the mines and steel plants, an all," Thompson added.

"People would get right off work, wouldn't even change clothes and come to the club to simply hear good music, dance and feel good about themselves. They wanted to have a good time and enjoy themselves in the process. That's why so many of us didn't mind playing in clubs that didn't pay much. It wasn't about the money. At least in the Black clubs we got some respect and some recognition."

Music hath charms
You bet she has,
But hasn't lent one yet to jazz

6

THE ROARING TWENTIES

The Roaring Twenties began as a war-weary city hoped for a "return to normalcy" after eighteen months of European combat in which more than 50,000 American died, including 1,500 from Pittsburgh. Warren G. Harding promised in his 1920 campaign slogan a "return to normalcy" that America would return to the values of prewar society if he was elected president.

That wasn't to be. Pittsburgh, like the rest of the nation, underwent cultural and social changes following World War I. Prohibition triggered the Jazz Age, which lasted from 1920 to the start of the Great Depression. Graft and public corruption ran rampant because of bootleggers and gangsters. There was so much illegal liquor in Pittsburgh that one law enforcement official said the city was "wet enough for rubber boots." Federal authorities were unable to stem the flow of illegal alcohol as cabarets opened where Black and white revelers danced together, triggering an outcry from religious and law enforcement officials.

Women gained the right to vote and experienced a sexual freedom that broke with traditional roles. They wore their dresses short, cut their hair in a bob, drank and smoked in public, went to speakeasies and were not the least embarrassed by their behavior. Birth control was available and allowed women to avoid unwanted pregnancies.

The nation's economy was booming, and jazz was growing in popularity despite efforts to stem the music's influence. Words like *sheik* and *flapper* were introduced into the lexicon along with the names Bix Beiderbecke and Paul

Whiteman. The Jazz Age easily could be called the "dance age," as new dances such as the Charleston, Black Bottom, the Trot and the Shimmy became the rage. Musicians had their own vernacular. An *axe* was a musical instrument. A *cat* was a musician, and a *gig* was a musical job.

It was jazz that made the Hill District a popular hangout and attracted national artists, who made visits to Pittsburgh a ritual. Mark Whitaker, author of *Smoketown: The Untold Story of the Other Great Black Renaissance*, writes that many southern migrants arriving in Pittsburgh were trained musicians who could play and read music. Their families found the city's public high schools included a rigorous music curriculum and prodded their children to take up an instrument when they entered school.

Pittsburgh became an important waypoint for jazz musicians shuttling between Chicago and New York City. The Hill District and East Liberty were stops for nationally known artists such as Duke Ellington, Count Basie, Fletcher Henderson, Billy Eckstine, Cab Calloway, Ella Fitzgerald, Noble Sissle, Chick Webb, Jimmie Lunceford and Lionel Hampton.

People flocked to speakeasies during Prohibition like the Paramount Inn, Little Paris the Kit Kat, Little Hollywood, the Rendezvous, the Peek Inn, the Delmont and the Royal Garden. Roadhouses also became popular, catering to crowds of young men seeking a chance to live life on the wild side with hip flasks, fast cars and faster women. The era also brought gangsters who peddled moonshine and operated the cabarets and roadhouses along with the advent of tabloid journalism, which feasted on the musical trends and violence that came with Prohibition.

Radio was in its infancy. Dr. Frank Conrad, an electrical engineer in Pittsburgh, became the so-called first disc jockey in America when he broadcast phonograph records in 1916 over a wireless radio set in a makeshift station in his garage. Station 8XK later became KDKA radio in 1920. Audiences began to gravitate to the music as more stations went on the air. By 1922, there were ninety stations operating in the country. Sales of radios that year totaled $60 million and reached $358 million two years later. By the end of the decade, sales of radios peaked at over $850 million, according to *The History of Jazz* by Ted Gioia.

Jazz enthusiasts couldn't get enough of the music and bought phonographs to listen to records. Songs recorded by Black artists, known in the vernacular at the time as "race records," attracted the attention of executives of newly formed recording companies. They forced radio stations to start playing jazz despite public criticism of the music. More than six thousand songs, featuring blues, gospel and jazz, had been produced, and by 1925, that figure increased to more than six million. The records helped musicians reach broader audiences since Black artists were barred from white-run clubs and dance venues. Enthusiasts could play the music in their homes or at parties or other social functions.

By 1927, more than 100 million records had been sold. People started going to cabarets and private clubs to hear live jazz. Newspaper ads touted music courses guaranteeing to teach a student to learn to play jazz in twenty lessons. The Charleston School of Music in Pittsburgh opened to teach the dance steps. Phonograph records gave way to juke boxes by 1930. The coin-operated machines began appearing in saloons, dance halls, restaurants and soda fountains after the repeal of Prohibition. Between 1933 and 1937, more than 150,000 juke boxes were manufactured, each holding fifty records. Jazz fans pumped nickels into the machines and played the same songs over and over. "Jazz was intoxicating," said saxophonist Don Aliquo Sr., eighty-nine, who began playing in Pittsburgh in 1956.

Pittsburgh bandleader Lois Deppe and pianist Earl "Fatha" Hines were the first Black musicians to play on radio when KDKA broadcast a program featuring Deppe and his Symphony Serenaders. There is some dispute about the exact date. Some reference works claim the event was broadcast in 1921. Others claim it was 1922. On August 5, 1922, the *Pittsburgh Press* reported on the broadcast with the headline, "Westinghouse Radio Program for Today."

"The broadcast created a lot of excitement especially in the colored neighborhood," Deppe said. On Wylie Avenue, one resident placed speakers from his crystal set on the porch so people could enjoy the music, according to Burton W. Peretti in *The Creation of Jazz. Music, Race and Culture in America.*

Hines played the piano while Deppe played the sax. They were accompanied by Vance Dixon on saxophone, Emmitt Jordon on violin, Oliver Saunder on the banjo, Thornton Brown on coronet, Harry Williams on drums and Henry Brasfield on trombone. In 1923, Hines recorded his first song, and five years later, he recorded eighteen songs with Louis Armstrong.

Dance clubs became enormously popular in the 1920s. Their popularity peaked in the late 1920s and reached into the early 1930s. Southern migrants, nostalgic for the food and music of home, flocked to cabarets in the 1920s eager for a taste of home cooking and jazz that was spreading across the nation.

Dozens of cabarets opened in the Hill District, East Liberty, the North Side and the downtown business district. Black and tan cabarets in the Hill District were filled with Black and white patrons who ate, drank and danced

Earl "Fatha" Hines moved from Pittsburgh to Chicago, where he placed in a nightclub owned by Al Capone. His recording with Louis Armstrong in the late 1920s, "Weatherbird," is considered a jazz classic. *Library of Congress.*

together, tearing down traditional racial barriers in a Pittsburgh that was highly segregated and unofficially followed Jim Crow laws.

Jazz musicians who played at these clubs attracted a following of female fans who threw notes onto the stage of a cabaret hoping a musician would see it and respond, wrote Charles Danver in a 1927 column in the *Pittsburgh Post.* One note came from "the blonde who sat at the corner table." Another was from "the girl in the red dress." One musician jokingly said he needed to hire a secretary to handle the twenty-five notes he received each week.

The cabarets caught the attention of public safety officials who were concerned about the relationships between Black and white people. In 1926, Pittsburgh passed a law regulating cabarets—requiring owners to obtain a dance license before three or more people could dance—but the real aim of the legislation was racial.

Police regularly raided cabarets, citing liquor law violations during Prohibition and for staying open past curfew, but it was white girls dancing with Black men that was the real motivation behind the raids. The *Pittsburgh Post* led a crusade against race mixing claiming that white teenage girls drank and danced with Black men. "In the resorts young white girls operate openly with negroes," reported the *Post* in 1925.

The newspaper also reported that white girls as young as fourteen were served alcohol and were seen drinking with Black men in the cabarets. Dr. Charles Zahnhiser, president of the Pittsburgh Council of Churches of Christ, said "indescribable orgies" were conducted inside the cabarets and that young white women were seen being carried out unconscious from cabarets. He also charged that police protected the brothels, gambling dens and bootleggers to ensure that a steady stream of protection money filled the coffers of politicians.

A local police chief lectured a group of white girls following a raid on one cabaret, telling them they should be ashamed to be in the company of Black men. "I'm not going to have any white girls coming to us and asking us to find the fathers of their dark-skinned babies," reported the *Pittsburgh Courier*, the city's Black newspaper, which also reported that city's Black clergymen railed against the comingling as well. Harry Collins, owner of the Collins Inn and later a jazz promoter, was hauled into court facing a revocation of his cabaret license because he allowed Black and white patrons to mingle, according to a 1922 article in the *Pittsburgh Post*.

No sooner had the music gripped the nation's frenzied youth than critics pounced, just as they would one day when rock 'n' roll, the Beatles and heavy metal came under criticism. Critics called jazz "evil," "primitive, "jungle music," "mental nausea" and "nothing but cheap and vulgar songs."

One educator, Dr. E.E. Overholtzer, told the *Pittsburgh Press* in 1924 that "the spirit of jazz has impregnated our National life. We dance to it, we sing to jazz, we eat to jazz and worst of all, our morals, our religion and our thoughts are turned to jazz."

The arrival of the Jazz Age in Pittsburgh didn't sit well with the city's clergy, especially the mainline Black ministers, who objected to the music. They blamed jazz for a decline in Sunday church attendance and a lessening of morals. They said the music, alcohol, soft lights and undulating movements of women amid the haze of cigarette smoke was more attractive than church.

"This is the code of pleasure," one minister complained to the *Pittsburgh Courier*. Some Black ministers objected to church choirs who took their skills into the community as performers and considered it "heathenistic behavior." Pittsburgh's Black middle class found the music vulgar. Father James Cox, a Catholic priest in Pittsburgh's Strip District, blamed the music for a decline in morality and making women and men more promiscuous. "Modern jazz from the beginning to end may be summoned up as jazz, jazz, jazz, a perfect example of discord in a discordant age," according to his biography, *The Mayor Shantytown: The Life of Father James Renshaw Cox*.

A Pittsburgh physician wrote in the *Pittsburgh Gazette Times* in 1917 that jazz was an illness that could be cured with sleep and regular meals. Mental health professionals linked jazz to an increase in hospital admissions. "I pity those poor souls in those hospitals who must sit and listen to a course of jazz," reported the *Pittsburgh Post*. The *Philadelphia Evening Ledger* reported in 1922 that civic organizations in Pittsburgh sent notices to concert venues asking them to play "two good numbers" each week to offset the effects of jazz.

"One jazz piece sounds like another," reported the *Pittsburgh Post* in 1925. "There is a thing as too much jazz. Play one [song] and you have practically played them all. King jazz is slipping. Jazz is soul food. Jazz is jungle music."

The *New York Sun* wrote in 1917 that jazz was the music of "contemporary savages." In 1921, the *Ladies Home Journal* claimed that jazz caused people to sin and destroyed brain cells, making it impossible for listeners to judge right from wrong and stimulated "the half-crazed barbarians to the vilest of deeds."

The Pennsylvania Federation of Women's Clubs held its annual convention in Pittsburgh in 1921 and proclaimed that jazz made people emotionally unbalanced "by a cacophony of woozy syncopation that combined to make jazz," reported the *Pittsburgh Post.* The federation also urged Congress to pass legislation banning jazz. People went to extremes to keep the music from being played.

Mayor Daniel Hart of Wilkes-Barre, Pennsylvania, banned the playing of jazz on public streets and required musicians to play only patriotic and classical music, according to the *Gazette Times* in 1924. John Brown University purchased the town of Sulphur Springs, Arkansas, so it could ban jazz and dancing in 1924, according to the *New York Times*. The *Times* also reported in the early '20s that Philadelphia wanted to ban jazz dancing altogether. New York wanted it banned in public places, and the City of Syracuse forbade couples from dancing under dim lights.

When Pittsburgh opened a new park in 1921, it banned the shimmy, toddle, face dancing "and other vulgar steps," reported the *Pittsburgh Sunday Post.* The American Society of Dancing Teachers wanted the federal government to create a board of censors to determine which dances were acceptable because jazz dances fostered degenerate behavior, they claimed.

A group of dance instructors asked Pittsburgh City Council to enact an ordinance banning couples from performing certain dances and would blacklist anybody wanting to perform these dances from all the city's dance academies. "I've run a dancing academy for a good many years but before I allow improper steps and holds go unreprimanded, I'll close up my places," F.J. Foreman told the *Gazette Times* in 1920. Fledgling radio stations were pressured to ban jazz from the airwaves. A listener wrote the *Pittsburgh Post* that "jazz is permissible on holidays but as a regular diet, it lacks nourishment." Despite the criticism, jazz slowly became accepted as serious music and gained in popularity. Jazz "has been ridiculed, distorted, fragmented, diluted, deemed unworthy of serious study," wrote pianist Billy Taylor.

Listening to jazz in a club or cabaret was akin to going to church. The music had to move you, unleash your soul. If musicians played the music well, the audience would embrace them. It was a sign of failure if the audience left before the musicians packed their instruments.

Pittsburgh's Hill District underwent a renaissance similar to the Harlem Renaissance in New York, which highlighted Black literature, culture, politics, art and music. The Hill also became the epicenter of Black art, music, sports, business and politics. The *Pittsburgh Courier* had sixteen regional editions and a circulation of 250,000, and Robert Vann, its founder and editor, was responsible for leading Black voters away from the GOP in 1932 and making them Democrats. The *Courier* also made boxer Joe Lewis and Jackie Robinson national heroes with its coverage. In sports, the Pittsburgh Crawfords was one of the leading teams in the National Negro League with Satchell Paige and Josh Gibson as major stars. Just across the Monongahela River in Homestead were the Pittsburgh Grays led by Cumberland Posey and Cool Papa Bell.

Music promoters helped establish Pittsburgh as a center for jazz, booking major acts that drew thousands. Gus Greenlee, Harry Collins, Birdie Dunlap, Sellers McKee Hall, Harry Hendel, Joe and Buzzy Robinson and Lenny Litman drew stars to their clubs. Greenlee was a bootlegger-turned-promoter-turned-sportsman who opened the famous Crawford Grill. Sellers McKee Hall opened the Pythian Temple and booked Fletcher Henderson and Benny Carter in 1928. Harry Collins hired Jelly Roll Morton to play at his Collins Inn, which he later sold to Greenlee, who renamed it the Paramount. It later became the Crawford Grill. Hendel owned the Roosevelt Theater and Savoy Ballroom. In 1936, as Pittsburgh was recovering from the 1936 St. Patrick's Day flood, more than 2,200 fans came to his Gold and Silver Ballroom to hear Louis Armstrong.

Jazz in Pittsburgh was here to stay.

7

SCHOOL DAYS

Westinghouse High School in Pittsburgh's Homewood neighborhood was no ordinary school. It was a music factory. The school's Wall of Fame includes jazz legends Billy Strayhorn, Erroll Garner, Ahmad Jamal, Grover Mitchell, Mary Lou Williams, Art Nance, Frank Cunimondo, Danny Conn and singer Dakota Staton along with Dr. Nelson Harrison, Linton Garner, Al Aarons, Danny Conn, Jerry Byrd, Clarence Oden, Wyatt Ruther, George Hudson and Warren Watson, a retired Pittsburgh judge.

The school's music program also produced talented classical musicians. Pianist Patricia Prattis Jennings and violinist Paul Ross were the first African Americans to join the Pittsburgh Symphony Orchestra. Jennings was hired by conductor William Steinberg, and in 1966, she was named principal keyboardist for the PSO. Ross signed a contract to play in 1965.

Westinghouse has also produced athletes who starred in the NFL and NBA along with graduates who became educators, physicians, artists and politicians. The school was a football powerhouse, winning the Pittsburgh City League Championship twenty-one straight years under the late football coach Pete Dimperio whose career record was 158-26-1.

Pittsburgh high schools have served as an incubator for the jazz world. Billy Eckstine and Dodo Marmarosa attended Peabody High School. Earl "Fatha" Hines, George Benson, Roy Brown, Stanley Turrentine and Walt Harper attended Schenley High School—so did bandleader and arranger Billy May, who later switched to composing for television and movies.

Left: Westinghouse High School turned out many great jazz artists who went on to fame. Many of the students were playing professionally by the time they entered Westinghouse. *Wikipedia.*

Right: Nelson Harrison, Dwayne Dolphin and Slide Hampton at Dowe's nightclub in Pittsburgh. *Courtesy of Nelson Harrison.*

Schenley High School Jazz Ensemble. Schenley, which opened in 1916, was the first school in the United States to cost over $1 million. *University of Pittsburgh Library System.*

Jazz musician and arranger Jerry Fielding, pianist David Budway and his sister Maureen came out of Taylor Allderdice High School. Singer Phyllis Hyman was a graduate of Carrick High School. Saxophonist Leo Pellegrino, known to his fans as "Leo P," graduated from the Creative and Performing Arts High School in the city's downtown cultural district and now is a musician in New York City. He also graduated from the Manhattan School of Music. Bassist Paul Thompson, also a CAPA graduate, toured with Maynard Ferguson and has played with George Benson, Slide Hampton, Jimmy Ponder, Stanley Turrentine and Roger Humphries, all Pittsburgh-bred musicians.

It was a tall music teacher with a rakish moustache that put Westinghouse on the musical map even though he never taught jazz. "I never called myself a jazz musician," said Carl McVicker in an oral history at Carnegie Library. "He was hired as a teacher and taught music for 34 years until retiring in 1961. He died in 1993 at the age of 89. McViker may not have been a performing jazz musician but he used jazz as a recruiting tool and continued to support students who wanted to play jazz."

Post-Gazette archives

Carl McVicker in 1956

jazz artists, but his former students also performed for big-city orchestras. Two of them, Ms. Jennings and Paul Ross, were the first black musicians hired by the Pittsburgh Symphony Orchestra in the mid-1960s.

In 1956, Westinghouse won the state orchestra championship. A dejected teacher from York whose orchestra had won the title in previous years said, "Let's get the hell out of here. No wonder that orchestra won. They all take lessons from the Pittsburgh Symphony."

Mr. Mac turned around and said, "Mister, I've got news for you. None of my people can afford to take lessons from the Pittsburgh Symphony. None."

He added, "My kids were lucky to have enough to eat."

*

Despite his singular role in music education, his record bears a stain that haunted him to his grave.

In 1936, the principal of Westinghouse, fearing the school might have its second black valedictorian in three years, told staff to lower the grade of Fannetta Nelson Gordon. Mr. Mac reluctantly changed her A in music to a B.

The erasure on her transcript still showed 75 years later. The Westinghouse Alumni Association recognized Ms. Nelson Gordon as valedictorian in 2011, three years after her death. Sophia Phillips Nelson, her sister and the first black valedictorian of Westinghouse, accepted the award for her

Carl McVicker. *Courtesy of Frank Cunimondo.*

When McVicker joined the faculty at Westinghouse, band was considered an activity and held only every two weeks. Music eventually became part of the curriculum. Frank Cunimondo was a student of McVicker who learned to play the sax after attending musical production at the school.

Cunimondo attended the after-school variety show and was unimpressed with the music until the house lights darkened and blue lights bathed the auditorium to the repetitive sound of drumbeats. The blue stage curtains slowly opened as an eighteen-piece student band began to play jazz before an audience of 1,800. "I got tears in my eyes. That's me," he said in an interview for this book. "I got to be in that band. I need to do this."

Cunimondo approached McVicker, who assigned him to learn the sax, and he eventually became good enough to be named to the K-Dets, an exclusive band composed of the best musicians in the school. "He was unbelievable," added Cunimondo about McVicker. "I owe my life to him."

Trombonist Nelson Harrison said many of McVicker's students were professional musicians by the time they reached high school but McVicker gave them a solid musical foundation, technical expertise, music theory, orchestration and encouragement. "We learned our jazz in the community. School had nothing to do with it," said Harrison in an interview. "I got

Top, left: Frank Cunimondo, in hat, in high school *Courtesy of Frank Cunimondo*. *Top, right*: High school photo of Frank Cunimondo at Westinghouse High School. *Courtesy of Frank Cunimondo*.

Bottom: Members of the K-Dets played the same arrangements as musicians in the Pittsburgh Symphony Orchestra. *Courtesy of Frank Cunimondo*.

schooled out on the streets where the masters were. He didn't teach jazz. He didn't play jazz. He never mentioned the world 'improvisation' but he was a wonderful guy."

The K-Dets were founded in 1946 by McVicker, but "it was always led by a student selected by the members, some of whom wrote charts for the band," Harrison said. "Mr. Mac bought the commercially available arrangements requested by the students from Volkwein's (music store). He did not direct the band musically but was the faculty sponsor. He was always a very encouraging faculty member and no doubt was able to offer performance opportunities for assemblies and other functions that wanted live music."

Members of the K-Dets over the years made their marks in the jazz world. In addition to Jamal and Harrison, Jerry Elliot, from the class of 1947, was a trombonist and arranger who recorded with Lester Young in 1947 and later toured with Ray Charles in the 1960s. Grover Mitchell graduated in 1948 and played with Count Basie and Duke Ellington along with trumpet player Al Aaron. Mitchell later led the Basie orchestra. Dakota Staton from the class of 1950 went onto become a major singing star.

McVicker had his students play the same arrangements that musicians did in the Pittsburgh Symphony Orchestra, according to Harrison, who studied under McVicker for two months before McVicker sent him for instruction to Matty Shiner at Duquesne University. Shiner was a nationally recognized trombonist who taught at the university for forty-six years.

The K-Dets were McVicker's creation, giving students interested in jazz more opportunities to perfom. *Courtesy of Frank Cunimondo.*

Dakota Staton recorded "The Late, Late Show" in 1957, and it made her a star. She was another in a long line of artists who graduated from Westinghouse High School. *Wikipedia.*

McVicker gave students a chance to perform in the school's three orchestras and swing band, which was unheard of at the time, since jazz was frowned on by educators. "Jazz was a dirty word then," McVicker said in a 1979 article in *Pittsburgh Magazine*. "The people in the educational system thought it was dangerous to encourage jazz bands but it was a way of interesting kids (in music)," he said.

"He was quite innovative," said Jamal in a 1995 radio interview on WKCR in New York. "He had four ensembles, the Beginners Orchestra, the Junior Orchestra and the Senior Orchestra, and then he started the K-Dets. It was unique, because this was the all-American Classical/Jazz band, and it was quite unusual for it to be in a high school at that time on such an organized basis."

In 1961, McVicker told the *Pittsburgh Press* that it was difficult during the Great Depression to persuade students to become involved in music when they were hungry and living in poverty. "We had no full-fledged music department. It was during the Depression and parents couldn't afford instruments or lessons."

On the first day of classes each year, McVicker would tell his music students "I don't care what religion you are, what sex or what race. It's how you blow that horn that counts with me," he recounted in *Pittsburgh Magazine*.

McVicker remembered Garner, Strayhorn and Jamal as students. "Erroll couldn't read music to play in the orchestra so he played tuba in the marching band and piano in the dance band," McVicker said in the Carnegie Library oral history. During a rehearsal, a pianist was having trouble making transitions in a song and another student recommended that McVicker give Garner a chance. "What's the use. He can't read music," McVicker said. He gave Garner a chance, and Garner played the song flawlessly. "Erroll, I don't care whether you can read music or not. You own this band from now on," McVicker told him.

Billy Strayhorn wrote two of Ellington's signature tunes, "Take the 'A' Train" and "Satin Doll." *Library of Congress.*

Another student, Freddie Jones, who later became Ahmad Jamal, was a professional at fourteen. "I had Ahmad Jamal when he was Freddie Jones and was so bashful, he would hide head in arms when asked to play," according to a 1961 *Pittsburgh Press* article.

As the musical reputation of the city's high schools grew, students clamored to enroll. Earl Hines, who lived south of the city, was sent by his parents to live with an aunt so he could attend Schenley High School. Lillian Strayhorn moved to an alley residence in Homewood so Billy could attend Westinghouse High School.

McVicker, born in 1904, played the trumpet and graduated from Edinboro State Teachers College and later Carnegie Institute of Technology. He was hired at Westinghouse as an instrumental music teacher when the enrollment was four hundred students. McVicker offered concert orchestra, marching band and the controversial swing band, the K-Dets. One roster included Ahmad Jamal and Grover Mitchell, Dakota Staton and Adam Wade on vocals, "Buzz" Renn (saxophone), Jack Renn (trombone) and trumpeters Danny Conn, Peter Henderson and Al Aarons.

McVicker's Orchestra Club included twenty-five of the best players chosen from the orchestra. This ensemble performed at society functions and at the homes of wealthy Pittsburgh residents. Wanting to be a classical pianist, Billy Strayhorn was the first African American member of the Orchestra Club.

Student performers also had to be serious and dedicated to the music craft. The curriculum encompassed theory, composition, orchestral practice and music fundamentals. Students were expected to blend and balance sound, understand key signatures and perform in a professional manner.

McVicker additionally taught brass instruments as a faculty member at the Pittsburgh Musical Institute. He was highly respected by his students and is recognized for encouraging students of all races and backgrounds to achieve. "Mr. McVicker instilled self-respect in those of us who were his students, because he respected us regardless of our background," Jamal said.

The Pittsburgh Musical Institute received its charter in 1915. The school, first located in Oakland on Fifth Avenue, was founded by Frank Milton Hunter, William H. Oetting, Charles N. Boyd and Dallmeyer Russell, all Western Pennsylvania natives. Boyd, credited as the co-founder and director, served as organ, composition and music theory instructor. In 1918, Boyd was elected president of the Music Teachers National Association, and in 1919, he founded the Pittsburgh Choral Society. In 1924, he was a founding member of the National Association of Schools of Music and Allied Arts, which currently accredits 625 college and university music programs.

The progressive school admitted African American musicians and counts among the alumni Strayhorn, Jamal and Vivian Reed, a Tony Award winner on Broadway, along with Walt Harper, Charles Austin, Carl Arter, Rubye Younge, composer Eddie Russ, bandleader George Hudson, Art Nance and classical music composers David Carey and Earl Wild.

Strayhorn was studying music theory and composition with Boyd at PMI when Boyd died in 1937. Strayhorn, in a 1962 interview in the *Pittsburgh Press*, said, "He was so wonderful, that I didn't think there was anyone else there who could teach me so I didn't stay."

At PMI's inception, a staff of eighteen teachers taught 150 students. They quickly outgrew the location and in 1921 moved to a larger building on Bellefield Avenue. This space, owned by PMI, housed thirty-two studio classrooms, a recital hall and three organs. The enrollment grew to 2,000 students and fifty-six teachers by 1928. Over eight hundred popular free recitals had been given by the PMI orchestra, chorus, senior and graduate students by that year.

Music students from all over the country applied and were admitted to PMI. By 1928, it had expanded and opened five small branch studio facilities in the city and twenty-eight in nearby towns, including Aliquippa, Ambridge, Bellevue, Butler, Canonsburg, Crafton, Monaca, Mount Lebanon and New Kensington. Auditions were held annually for high school students seeking admission. The University of Pittsburgh and PMI exchanged credits under an agreement, and after World War II many military musicians attended PMI using the GI bill. PMI merged with the University of Pittsburgh music department in 1963.

The Mary Cardwell Dawson School of Music opened in Homewood in 1927. Among its students were Ahmad Jamal and Joe Kennedy Jr., who later became a violinist with the Richmond Symphony Orchestra. Dawson was an opera singer who created the National Negro Opera Company in 1941. "Mary Cardwell Dawson was a terrific music educator," recalled Kennedy in an interview with the Jazz Preservation Society. "My mother would take me by the hand to lessons." He was boyhood friends with Jamal. "Ahmad and I would play at class recitals and church. It was a wonderful, wonderful memory."

Fillion Studios opened in Oakland in 1925 under founder Ferdinand Fillion and eventually had a staff of seventy music instructors. Among its notable graduates was Dakota Staton.

No matter how good a Black musician could play, white audiences still viewed them derisively. Pete Henderson, a trumpet player who attended Westinghouse High School with Jamal, whom he remembered as Fritzie Jones, said they went to a downtown music story to buy a book on piano theory. The white clerk looked at Jamal and said, "What do you want a book for?" Henderson told the clerk that Jamal was no ordinary musician. There was a piano in the center of the store, and Jamal sat down and began playing. The clerk was "flabbergasted." Customers began crowding around the piano to listen to Jamal. "The white attitude was niggers don't know nothin'," Henderson said in an interview with the African American Jazz Preservation Society. "Fritzie lit up the place."

8
THE ECONOMICS OF JAZZ

Carl Arter earned thirty-five cents an hour working at Isaly's, a popular dairy and restaurant chain with stores in Pittsburgh and throughout Allegheny County. He worked there because he couldn't earn a living playing jazz. Working a day job was part of the life and sacrifice of being a musician. If you wanted to play jazz, you had to work because the earnings from a musical career wasn't enough to support a family.

"You were making $30 a week, you were makin' a lot of money," said Arter in an interview at the Maurice Levy Oral History Collection at the Carnegie Library in Pittsburgh.

African American musicians couldn't play in white-run downtown clubs, so Arter was relegated to play in "ghetto clubs" in the Hill District and other Black neighborhoods where the hours were long but the pay was higher. Being a musician "ain't like a job punching a time clock," he said.

Racism and segregation limited job opportunities for Black musicians as late as the 1970s. Arter and other musicians were forced to work full-time jobs as truck drivers, as elevator operators at department stores or car salesmen or, in the case of Will Austin, working thirty-five years for the U.S. Postal Service. Bassist Marcus Kelly said the pay scale under the musicians' union contract wasn't enough to support a family when a nightclub paid only eighty-five dollars split between five musicians. "If you don't have a day job you can't turn down an offer to play," said Kelly in a Carnegie Library interview. "So, you didn't complain about whether you are paid union scale."

Trombonist Tommy Turk was the leader of the popular Deuces Wild jazz combo in the late 1940s and 1950s. He had a national reputation as a musician but as a husband and father of two boys, he barely made ends meet, according to a 1953, article in the *Pittsburgh Press*. His annual salary for that year was $5,500. Turk eventually moved Las Vegas where he earned more money playing in the house bands at gambling casinos until he was murdered in a liquor store robbery. Fellow Deuces Wild sidemen drummer Carl Peticca gave music lessons while bassist Danny Mastri was a barber.

Sax player George Thompson was proud of being a musician, but the job didn't put bread on the table. When he tried to buy furniture on credit, the salesman asked for his occupation for his credit application. "I'm a musician," Thompson said in an interview at the African American Jazz Preservation Society. "I was proud of being a musician. Yes, I would do it again. I love the music." It was then he realized there was no way he would be able to buy the furniture so Thompson got a job at demolition company tearing

Frank Cunimondo at piano. *Courtesy of Frank Cunimondo.*

down buildings, but the work left him exhausted. Once he was dismantling a building when he leaned against a wall on the eighteenth floor and fell asleep because he was so tired. He awoke in time before he nearly fell.

Jazz in Pittsburgh created an entire economy. Cabarets and nightclubs opened and were filled with people eating and drinking. Musicians played six nights a week. "I don't know of any places that play six nights a week anymore," said pianist Frank Cunimondo in an interview. Musicians sold records. Stores sold instruments and sheet music. Technicians repaired broken instruments. Pianos needed tuners. Hotels provided rooms for touring musicians, and restaurants fed them. Marketing representatives touted the talent of their artists. Booking agents were busy, and live concerts raked in money for promoters. Music schools opened to teach children. Work crews were needed to set up stages for touring musicians who played in Pittsburgh. Sidemen were hired to back up or fill in for visiting bands.

The jazz economy in the city went bust because of urban renewal in the Hill District and in East Liberty, forcing clubs to close because of the changing face of the neighborhoods. The loss of nightclubs forced musicians to take day jobs. Band leaders hired the musicians they needed for a performance or allowed club owners and booking agents to do the hiring. Club owners also exploited musicians by refusing to pay them union scale—since jobs were scarce, the artists seldom complained. Musicians playing at mob-run clubs were afraid to complain if they were short-changed since they knew what the penalty would be if they did.

Drummer Roger Humphries said younger musicians didn't realize how difficult it was to work full-time as a musician because they didn't understand the economics of the music industry. "Here in Pittsburgh, guys will say I'm a musician and that's all I'm going to do. I'm going to make a living. It's a tough road to hoe and make a living in Pittsburgh as a sideman. You've got to have a job," he said in an interview with the Carnegie Library.

Jazz musicians who are members of the American Federation of Musicians earned an average salary of $37,200 in 2012, according to a survey by the Future of Music Coalition. The earnings of jazz artists usually depend on negotiating an amount of money directly with the club owners who hire them. If they are hired as sidemen, then they must be paid union scale, which calls for a payment of $115 for a job that lasts three hours or less, according the 2019 contract of Local 60-471 of the American Federation of Musicians in Pittsburgh. Rehearsals fees require a payment of $99.50 for a minimum of three hours or less and $19.00 for every quarter of an hour of overtime.

Orchestral musicians can earn much more than a jazz player, according to a study by the Berklee College of Music in Boston. "Music Careers in Dollars and Cents" reported symphony musicians earn between $28,000 and $143,000 annually in some cities. Pit musicians on Broadway earn between $800 and $1,500 weekly, according to the study.

The Music Industry Research Association and the Princeton University Survey Research Center released a study in 2018 that found the median salary for musicians in 2017 was between $20,000 and $25,000 annually. Most of a musician's earnings—81 percent—came from live performances, followed by teaching at 42 percent. Musicians received minimal revenue from streaming services and the sale of merchandise at concerts.

Older musicians nearing retirement fear they will not be able to support themselves after they quit performing. The Jazz Foundation of America has a Musicians Emergency Fund to help artists who have fallen on hard times. The fund helps provide free medical help, disaster relief assistance and finding housing for musicians who have no place to live.

Trumpet player Danny Conn worked as a musician all his life and never had another job. He played in nightclubs, with Claude Thornhill and Stan Kenton and toured everywhere from Hattiesburg, Mississippi, to Chicago and San Francisco. He even played in strip clubs. "I probably played millions of notes at a nickel a note," he said in a Carnegie Library interview.

In an interview, Don Aliquo Sr. said Conn never seemed to stop working. "He had seven or eight kids. He made a living. That was no mean feat."

Cunimondo also never worked a daytime job in his career but made enough money to work full-time as a musician; now at eighty-five, he teaches and performs. "I was blessed all my life," he said in an interview. "I thank God all the time for that. I thank God for making me a musician. If you want to be a musician you have to make sacrifices. You don't have job security. You don't have benefits and it's difficult to get financial support."

9

JESUS WASHED MY SINS AWAY

Dr. James Johnson's father was unhappy when his son told him he wanted to be a jazz musician. His father and all his uncles were ministers. Johnson grew up in the Christian Methodist Episcopal Church and understood better than most musicians the relationship between jazz and gospel music. To Johnson, there was no difference, according to an interview in the jazz oral history collection at the Manchester Craftsmen's Guild in Pittsburgh.

"When I heard the word 'Jesus' in 'Jesus washed my sins away,' I said stop, stop, stop. This is a religious song." Someone corrected him and explained the connection between gospel music and jazz. "We were witnessing a merger of jazz, blues and gospel all into one form," said Johnson, who runs the Afro American Music Institute in the Homewood neighborhood of Pittsburgh. "I'd be playing at a jazz club on Saturday night and play at the church on Sunday morning. Same licks. Hands go up."

Improvisation is the link between jazz and gospel music, wrote Idella Lulamae Johnson in her 2009 doctoral dissertation, "Development of African American Gospel Piano Style (1926–1960): A Socio-Musical Analysis of Arizona Dranes and Thomas A. Dorsey" at the University of Pittsburgh. Thomas A. Dorsey, considered "the father of Black gospel music," had a background in jazz and blues and wrote songs for Ethel Waters and Bessie Smith before turning his full attention to gospel. Arizona Dranes was a blind female pianist who injected ragtime and boogie woogie into gospel tunes.

Gospel music has roots in the blues, ragtime, boogie woogie and jazz, wrote Johnson. The music played in Black church services, along with singing, relies on improvisation just like jazz does. She said gospel music "has the same plaintive quality of the blues, the energy of ragtime and barrelhouse, the persistence of boogie woogie and the grace of jazz." Jazz has been shaped by an understanding of jazz harmony and piano techniques common to both genres.

People attending Hill District church services on a Sunday morning may have heard a mix of the blues, jazz and Baptist hymns along with dancing, spontaneous singing and improvisation much like a jazz band might employ in a nightclub, according to Johnson's 2009 study. Baptist spirituals were a form of response to the oppressive conditions experienced by Black people in America. The songs expressed the desire of slaves for spiritual as well as physical freedom. The spirituals provided enslaved people with a way to express their feelings in both text and melody.

In the 1930s and 1940s, there were forty-five churches in the Hill District, many of them storefront churches whose services were a hybrid of traditional worship mixed with loud and long bursts of praise and emotion, according to *City at the Point: Essays on the Social History of Pittsburgh*, published by the University of Pittsburgh Press.

These storefront churches were housed in former commercial buildings that had been abandoned and allowed to deteriorate. Service times were written outside the buildings in chalk or paint with a sign welcoming people of all races. Southern migrants felt unwelcome in long-established Black Hill District residents and their more traditional forms of worship so they began attending these more vibrant, spiritual services at storefront churches.

"When musicians would jam all night, they would walk down the sidewalks, the city sidewalks, then there would be a storefront church service going on. They would walk in with their instruments and they did not check that jazz and blues music at the door," James Johnson continued. "This is how we get jazz in the church cause a lot of them (church musicians) were actually jazz musicians. A lot of them were blues musicians. A lot of them would be up all night and they'd go right from the jam session to the church but the music remained the same. To all it sounded like jazz. You were running a jazz line. It's the same spirit. It's the spirit of the music."

Children playing outside in the Hill District on every day of the week were lured into the church by the musical mixture of gospel, blues and jazzy improvisational style of Baptist music. Saxophonist Art Nance, in another Manchester Craftsmen's Guild interview, said he came from a religious family and attended church services six nights a week and all day on Sunday. Nance remembers that shouting and "funky" music that was part of the worship.

Drummer Chuck Spadafore lived in the Hill District as a boy and listened to the music coming from the storefront churches along Wylie Avenue. "I was born on the Hill and I think that's where I got my sense or feel for the blues. I used to go to the revivals up the street from where I lived. There was a black church right on the corner on Bedford and Elm. We'd be playing outside and would hear the music and go in. Where else would I have heard that type of music?" said Spadafore in "Crossroads of the World," a doctoral dissertation by Colter Harper at the University of Pittsburgh.

When Black migrants reached the Hill District, there was little interest by long-established Black residents in their culture or music. The newcomers brought songs from slave days that contained African American melodies and rhythms that native Black Pittsburghers found offensive, according to "When Gospel Music Sparked a 'Worship War'" in a 2018 article in *Christianity Today*. But as Black church attendance declined, the clergy grudgingly allowed southern gospel music in their services.

"If we had been born free, there would have been no gospel songs," wrote Pittsburgh gospel singer Anna Murrell in an article written for the *Pittsburgh Courier* in 1966. "But born into bondage, much of this music was dedicated to death and an early release from slavery."

Negro spirituals during the era of slavery were used to teach, scold and speak of deliverance from slavery. It was a way of communicating through music they used at work, in leisure times and in religious services. At the conclusion of a religious ceremony, congregants formed a circle and began shuffling in a jerking motion while singing and dancing. One person might be thrust into the middle where the singing and dancing continued.

Frank Bolden, editor of the *Pittsburgh Courier*, said most of the young women and girls living on the Hill could sing and play the piano because Baptist churches had a major influence on music in the Hill District. Gospel music got people off the pews and into the aisles clapping and singing. Instrumental music added to the lively mix with dancing, prayer and more vocal music at lengthy services. Many children who later played jazz were exposed to gospel music through church attendance.

Church music has been intertwined with jazz in the Hill District ever since the Great Black Migration saw African Americans moving north. The church was the adhesive that held groups together as they traveled. The clergy had no choice but to migrate as well, to reestablish congregations at the new location.

Black church services were composed, in part, of call and response singing that melodically and harmonically resembled the blues. The physicality of the worship further added to the spirit, including dancing, clapping, swaying, stomping and moving into the aisles much like "praise houses" in the South.

Every established church had a vocal choir to assist in leading worship and competed with one another to be the best. The vocal choirs understood and worshiped in the gospel style that had similarities with ragtime and blues. Black choir members also formed singing groups outside the church and sang at public events, further exposing the bluesy, swinging style of gospel music.

After urban renewal began in the 1950s, Black residents in the Hill moved to the suburbs, and church music was on the wane. Parishioners stopped attending their home churches as they were forced to move to make way for the Civic Arena. Baptists became Methodists and Episcopalians, and church services were never so lively as in the Baptist churches, recounted Frank Bolden, editor of the *Pittsburgh Courier*, in a Carnegie Library interview. Bolden said a former Hill resident who moved to Penn Hills told him church services were boring because "white people can't sing a lick."

The Baptist denomination invested almost three quarters of a million dollars in the twenty-nine organizations under its broad banner. There were fourteen traditional Black churches in the Hill District, including several Black Baptist churches, Saint James Church and Ebenezer Baptist.

Macedonia Baptist Church, Bedford Avenue, Hill District. There was little difference between the music played on Saturday night at jazz clubs and the gospel tunes at church services on Sunday mornings. *University of Pittsburgh Library System.*

The Ebenezer Baptist Church on Wylie Avenue was established in August 1875. By 1900, 600 members had reduced their debt from $23,000 to $12,000. The congregation was debt-free by 1908. Between 1902 and 1915, membership increased from 772 to 1,500 members, and theirs was the first Black Baptist church to pay missionaries for foreign field work. Membership continued to increase, and by 1926, the congregation numbered 2,000, largely due to immigration and the need for labor in the steel and iron industries.

Membership remained high into the 1940s, with 2,000 members and 200 children in the under fifteen years of age youth program. The church's influence in the community was enormous. One congregant noted, "The spirit of God works upon you in different ways. At camp meetings there must be a ring shout here, a ring shout there, a ring shout over yonder, or sinners will not be converted."

James Johnson said the "Black church is what kept Black people together. It was the only place where they could express themselves without fear of some type of reprisal without being threatened."

10

THE MERGE

In the 1970s, a group of disgruntled Black jazz musicians tried to tear away, what they charged, was an invisible racial barrier that prevented Black artists from performing at white-owned downtown nightclubs and other high-profile concert venues because of discrimination. The Black Musicians of Pittsburgh filed a lawsuit in 1971 in federal court challenging the 1965 merger between Black Local 471 and the white Local 60 of the American Federation of Musicians claiming the white-led union was preventing African American artists from playing at white clubs where the fees were higher.

The plaintiffs wanted the five-year time limit of the merger extended, hiring quotas put in place and punitive damages paid to the Black Musicians of Pittsburgh. The litigation was triggered after a complaint was filed with the Equal Employment Opportunity Commission by George Childress, who served as business agent for Local 471 before the consolidation. The EEOC investigated the allegations and reported that Local 60-471 had engaged in "the most pervasive and severe racially discriminating practices," according to the commission's legal brief. The commission issued a right to sue letter in 1972, which allowed the BMOP to initiate legal action.

Childress, who died before the lawsuit was litigated, appeared before the executive board Local 60-471 and complained that Black members were restricted to playing at "ghetto clubs and dances" and accused white union officials of "a long vicious record of racial injustice."

Membership cards for drummer Art Blakey. He was a member of Local 471 of the American Federation of Musicians. *African American Jazz Preservation Society, University of Pittsburgh Library System.*

"Since the expiration of the merger agreement, Blacks have been unable to obtain any position of leadership within the merged union.…The union has discriminated against the Blacks in the terms of job opportunities. When requests are made to the union for musicians, the requesting parties are always referred to white musicians," according to EEOC records.

The BMOP hired attorney William Gould, a law professor at Stanford University's law school, to press their case. Gould was the great-grandson of an escaped slave who served in the Union navy during the Civil War. He became the first Black professor hired at Stanford's law school and also served in the mid-90s as chairman of the National Labor Relations Board. Gould had won a $5.3 million settlement in a racial discrimination case against Detroit Edison in 1971 over the hiring and promotion of African American workers.

"Blacks have been systematically excluded from better paying jobs downtown in clubs and hotels," Gould told the *Pittsburgh Courier*. "We want, first of all, to set up an effective hiring path or quota system. We've also been excluded from political positions within the union; we'd like the court to reinstate the plan which existed after 1965 with an equal share of Blacks on the union's executive board."

"To add insult to injury once the merger was complete, the effects of past discrimination continues when so many Black musicians lost tenure, union time or benefits," added drummer Harold Lee in an interview with the African American Jazz Preservation Society.

The passage of the Civil Rights Act of 1964 paved the way for the merger of Black and white union locals across the country. Under the terms of the consolidation, which Black members referred to as "the merge," the union's executive board would consist of nine members. Six would come from Local 60 and three from Local 471.

The newly merged union would be permitted to hire a Black office worker under the terms of the five-year deal. After that time expired, Black and white musicians would be on equal footing with no quotas and vote for whoever—Black or white—they wanted as officers or members of the board of directors. But since Black members were outnumbered, 2,000 to 324, Austin said they were unable to elect one of their own to any elective office and therefore had "no Black voice within Local 60-471."

The aftermath of the merger was marked by bitterness. Local 471 officials turned over their membership records to Local 60, which were then lost or burned, causing older Black members to lose their insurance and death benefits that they had held for decades. In order to get benefits, the Black members had no way to prove their membership. "It's a crying shame. It just hurts," Austin said in a letter contained in Local 471 archives. "We expected a more level playing field. But that didn't happen."

Organist Rubye Younge complained to the union's executive board in June 1973 about its treatment of Childress. "No real man would treat another person in this manner when he is flat on his back," according to a letter in union records. She accused white union officials of "blatant racism. Our local had to fight to maintain our human dignity. 'They didn't want us and we didn't want them,'" she said.

The principal witness in the trial was Carl Arter, former president of Local 471, who testified that white union members wanted no part of Black musicians in the newly formed union. Arter said the aim of the lawsuit was equality. "I wanted to protect any type of relationship I could at the same time improve conditions for all musicians, not just the black ones," according to the trial transcript.

Arter told the court how he once tried to enter the white social club of Local 60 before the merger with two white musicians but was told the club was for white members only. "I didn't want to make any trouble. I just left," said Arter according to transcript of trial testimony in a 1971 lawsuit filed by the BMOP against Local 60-471 contained in the files of the American Civil Liberties Union.

In another incident with racial overtones, Arter testified that white union officials did what they could to prevent Black musicians from performing downtown, where many jazz clubs were located. He cited an incident in 1954 when Arter and other Black artists were hired to play at the opening of the New Nixon Café and Supper Club downtown. White members of Local 60 picketed the club, charging that Arter had infringed on Local 60's territory and defied a union ban that prevented Black musicians from playing in clubs along Grant Street. As a result, Arter was suspended from the union and fined $500.

It took Arter a decade to pay the fine. "White people are not ready for us blacks and politically we were not ready to cope with Local 60," added Arter. He also testified that Black members failed to use the union's grievance system because they knew that if they did, they would face a "hostile white board" and "cold hostility." They realized they were "not going to get a fair shot."

Younge testified at the federal trial that she had been sent on three job interviews by a white Local 60-471 official only to learn the jobs had already been filled by the same white official who initially told her about the potential job openings.

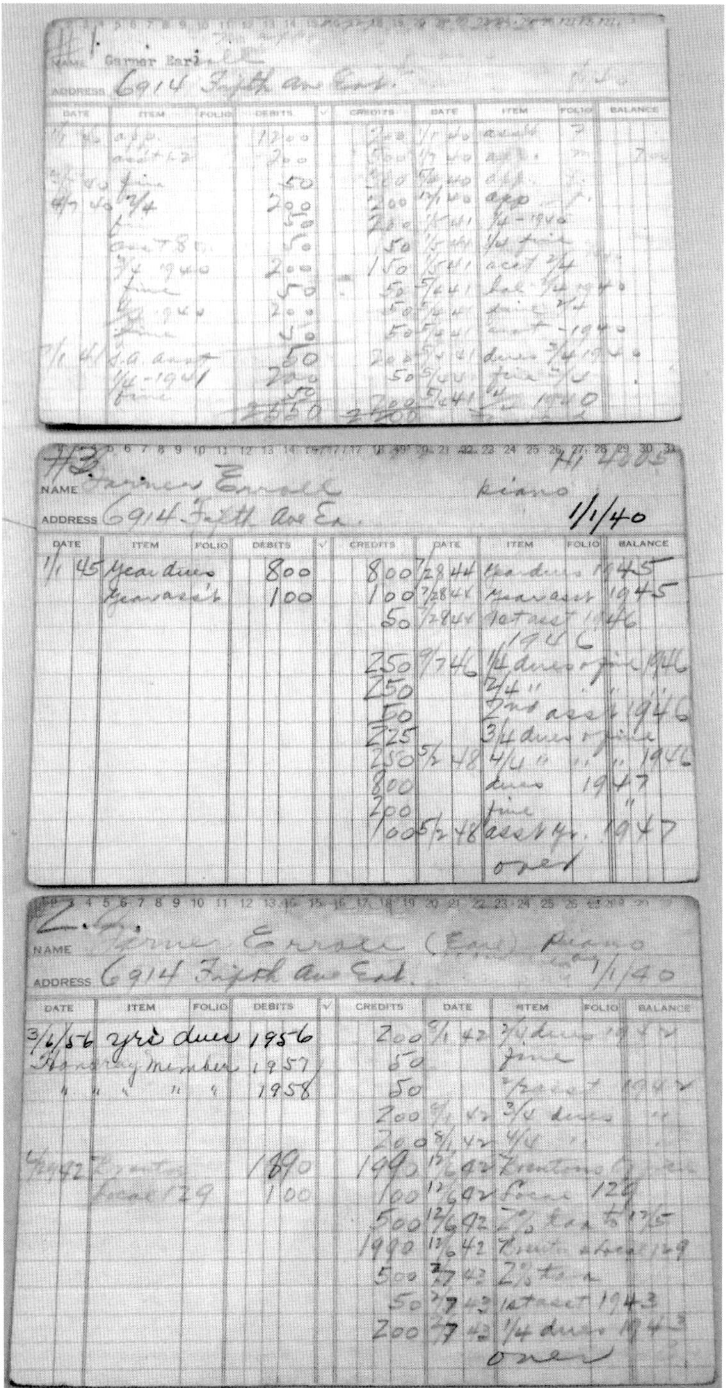

NAME Garner Earl
ADDRESS 6914 Fifth Ave Ext.
DATE ITEM FOLIO DEBITS CREDITS DATE ITEM FOLIO BALANCE
NAME Garner Erroll piano
ADDRESS 6914 Fifth Ave Ex. 1/1/40
Year dues
NAME Garner Erroll (Earl) piano
ADDRESS 6914 Fifth Ave Ext. 1/1/40
yrs dues 1956
Honorary member 1957
1958

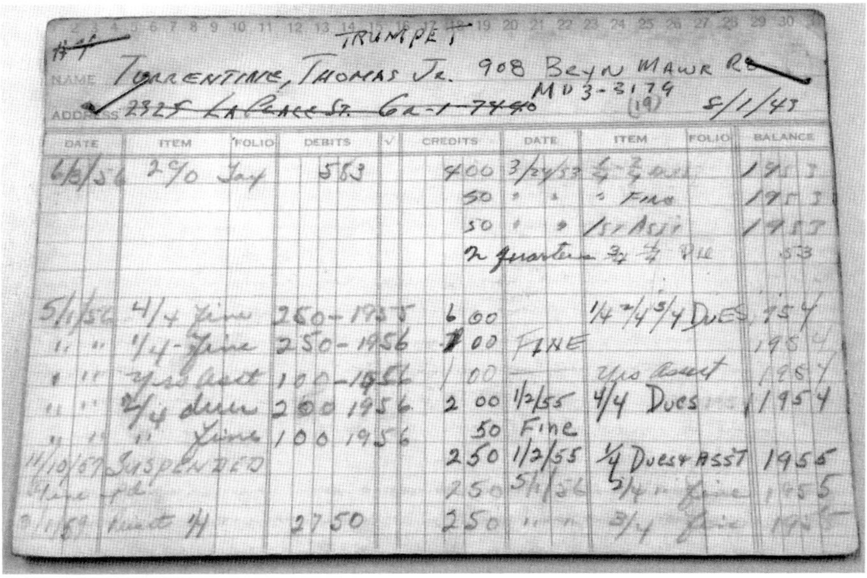

Opposite: Erroll Garner union cards. Garner was unable to read music, a requirement to join the union, but Local 471 made an exception for Garner because of his talent. *African American Jazz Preservation Society, University of Pittsburgh Library System.*

Above: Tommy Turrentine union cards. Tommy Turrentine was an accomplished trumpet player but never achieved the fame that his brother saxophonist Stanley Turrentine received. *African American Jazz Preservation Oral History Project, University of Pittsburgh Library System.*

Bassist Bobby Boswell testified that white union officials persuaded him to run for a position on the executive board to undercut the lawsuit. "I began to feel that I was being used because they needed a black man on the board and if you one you can say, 'We have one and we are not slighting anyone,'" testified Boswell, according to the trial transcript. "And, I could have won the election easily."

Drummer Roger Humphries, who was a member of an ad hoc committee of the Black Musicians of Pittsburgh, said he knew the lawsuit would be unsuccessful. "I was glad I did what I did but I didn't need no union shit," he said.

Pianist George Duke Spaulding opposed the merger because neither side wanted to be part of the other, according to an interview with the African American Jazz Preservation Society. He said Black members had unreasonable expectations about the benefits the merger would provide. Instead of more opportunities to play in upscale white venues, Black artists were still stymied in gaining engagements in white clubs.

Saxophonist George Thompson said the merger further isolated Black musicians from reaching white audiences so Black musicians of the newly merged local 60-471 stopped attending meetings, stopped paying dues and stopped voting in union elections. "I knew it was a mistake that we made. Even though it happened it still held us back," he said in an interview with the Jazz Preservation Society. "We were isolated in areas we had to play in."

Pianist Walt Harper complained about the racial barrier erected by white member. "Although Local 471 attempted to force issues weakly, it simply could not penetrate downtown," Harper said. Drummer Cecil Brooke said many 471 members quit the union in disgust because of the local's inability to fight racism. "The reality is that Local 471 never had a chance to really reach its full potential," said drummer Curtis Young.

Austin said Black musicians hurt themselves by refusing to attend meetings and adapting to new music that audiences wanted to hear. Many union issues, he said, were decided by slim margins, and if two or three more Black union members had showed up to vote, their position within the union may have been different. "I can understand the frustration of a lot of the guys because they just didn't participate," Austin said in a history of Local 471 in the archives at the University of Pittsburgh. Another problem facing Black musicians was the fact that white nightclub owners sat on the executive board of Local 60-471 and blackballed certain African American musicians from their businesses.

Despite the findings by the EEOC and hearing testimony from Black artists, Judge Barron McCune ruled Local 60-471 did not discriminate and that Black candidates for elective office had just as much chance at winning at seat on the board as white members if only more Black musicians had been active in the union. He noted that Black members routinely boycotted elections and did not participate in other union affairs.

In his ruling, he wrote, "The record shows that black members can win elections and that social intercourse and friendship can develop and become common place. It will require efforts on both sides and a combined effort has been lacking," according to order. As to the issue of performance fees, McCune found that an analysis of union records revealed African American musicians were making more money than their white counterparts.

The BMOP unsuccessfully appealed McCune's ruling to the U.S. Third Circuit Court of Appeals and then to the U.S. Supreme Court, which declined to hear the case. Attorney William Gould was stunned by the decision. "I am most disappointed….The situation vis-à-vis the union is a lost cause from a legal point of view," he said in *Jazz and Justice: Racism and the Political Economy of Music.*

Hal Davis, who was union president in 1970, said he was committed to electing more Black musicians to the executive board because it would be a mistake to have a "lily white" administration and urged white members to support Black candidates for office, according to a letter contained in the union's archives.

Guitarist Joe Negri, who was known as the character Handyman Negri on the public television show *Mister Rogers' Neighborhood*, downplayed the racial tension between the two sides and said Black and white musicians were united by their love of the music. "I don't think we were that divided," he said in an interview. "There was division. I wouldn't call it a racial tension. I guess it was the way life was then. We were a little bit divided but we were all friendly. We did things together and even recorded together." Saxophonist Don Aliquo Sr. said some Black musicians were not hired to perform downtown because they could not read music. "Most of the work required the ability to read music and some Black artists didn't read music well."

The segregation of Black musicians stems from an obscure agreement that few musicians even knew existed. The Afro-American Musical Association was an early group of professional, classically trained musicians who were viewed as inferior by white musicians and barred from performing in the symphony, opera or other public functions where whites would be in the audience.

The Afro-American Musical Agreement between white and Black musicians was signed in 1906. Two years later, Local 471 was formed. The separation of the two races in the musical world remained in effect until 1964, when civil rights legislation forced Black and white unions across the country to merge. Federal law no longer allowed separate union locals for Black and white workers within the same industry.

Afro-American Musical Association of Pittsburgh was formed by Black artists who voluntarily signed the agreement that restricted them from performing in clubs and other social functions within white-dominated areas of the city. But the real purpose of the deal was to keep Black musicians from playing in white parts of Pittsburgh at a time when segregation and Jim Crow rules were in effect to maintain barriers "designed to ensure free-born Blacks and ex-slaves would not obtain economic or social parity with whites," according to Local 471 archives.

Drummer Curtis Young said these early musicians were not jazz artists but were classically trained. "During this period, Black musicians were struggling to gain and maintain a measure of respect from a hostile white society convinced they were inferior," he recounted in an interview housed in the Maurice Levy Jazz Oral History collection at the Carnegie Library. "The original members were the real pioneers and were considered professional because they focused on the classical music style and did not play jazz. These musicians could read music, were formally trained in their instruments and maintained a performance demeanor that did not allow for improvisation."

A history of the association, contained in the archives of Local 471 held by the University of Pittsburgh, said early Black musicians in Pittsburgh had to fight to gain a measure of respect "from a hostile white society convinced of their inferiority." Young said these early Black artists were "real pioneers" but did not play jazz "because they focused on the classical music style....These musicians could read music, were formally trained in their instruments and maintained a performance demeanor that did not allow for improvisation spontaneity, or versatility of jazz." His thoughts were recorded in an interview maintained by Carnegie Library in the Maurice Levy Jazz Oral History Collection.

Black musicians were humiliated by white music promoters who placed restrictions on Black artists whenever they performed with white musicians or accompanied white women singers, according to "Jazz and Racism in the USA during Jim Crow," by Silvia Escribano Delgado. For a time, Black and white musicians could not perform together at all. If a white woman was on stage with Black musicians, the Black men had to wear masks, according to the study.

When bandleader Artie Shaw hired a Black trumpet player to tour with his orchestra in the South, promoters insisted the musician be at least fifteen feet apart from any white artists, according to the essay, "Tough on Black Asses: Segregation Ideology in Early American Jazz History," published in Historical Perspectives at the University of California at Santa Barbara. If the skin tone of Black musicians was too dark, promoters forced them to apply white powder to their faces before playing before a white audience in order not to offend white sensibilities.

Black musicians could play only at clubs in the Black neighborhoods in the Hill District, East Liberty and the North Side—known as the 'chitlin circuit—while white artists would could play in the rest of Pittsburgh or with the Pittsburgh Symphony or opera company. Black composer Robert Nathaniel Dett lamented the lack of opportunity for Black musicians in the United States in a 1918 article in the magazine, "Musical America": "We have this wonderful store of folk music—the melodies of an enslaved people who poured out their longings, their grief and their aspiration in one great, universal language."

The membership of Local 471 included legends in the jazz world. The union's archives contain union cards for drummer Art Blakey, bassist Ray Brown, saxophonist Stanley Turrentine, trumpet player Roy Eldridge, pianists Erroll Garner, Walt Harper, Horace Parlan, Alyce Brooks and Mary Lou Williams. Trombonists Nelson Harris and Grover Mitchell, who both went on to play with the Count Basie Orchestra, were union members.

Local 471 was considered a subsidiary of Local 60 until the merger. These segregated organizations were allowed to exist ever since the U.S. Supreme Court ruled in *Plessy v. Ferguson* in 1896 that racial segregation did not violate the Fourteenth Amendment guaranteeing individuals equal protection under the law as long as the facilities for were equal. But the effect of the *Plessy* decision was to relegate Black performers to second-class status in the music field. There were about fifty or so Jim Crow locals in the country besides Pittsburgh. Denver, Atlantic City, Chicago, Philadelphia, Cleveland, Milwaukee, Boston and Washington, D.C., were among cities targeted for mergers. The American Federation of Musicians realized the time was coming when racial barriers would be torn down, but

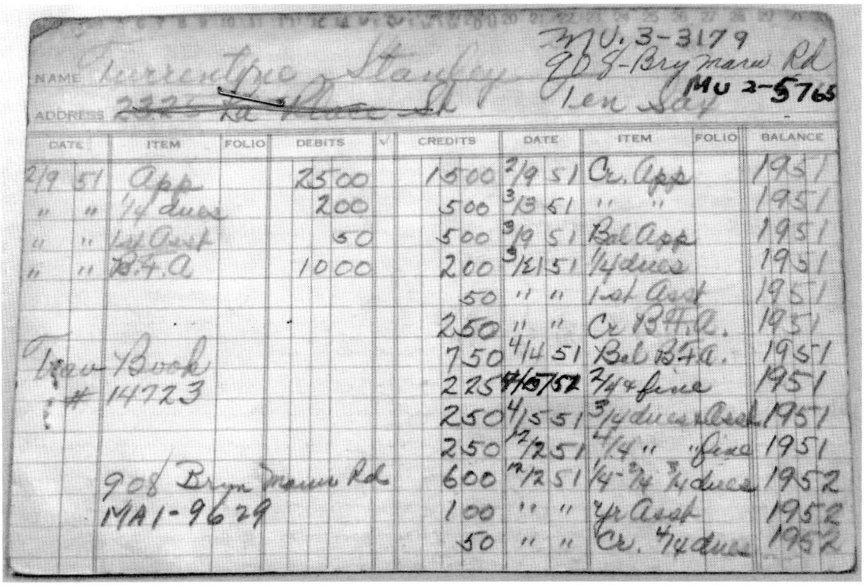

Stanley Turrentine union card. *African American Jazz Preservation Society, University of Pittsburgh Library System.*

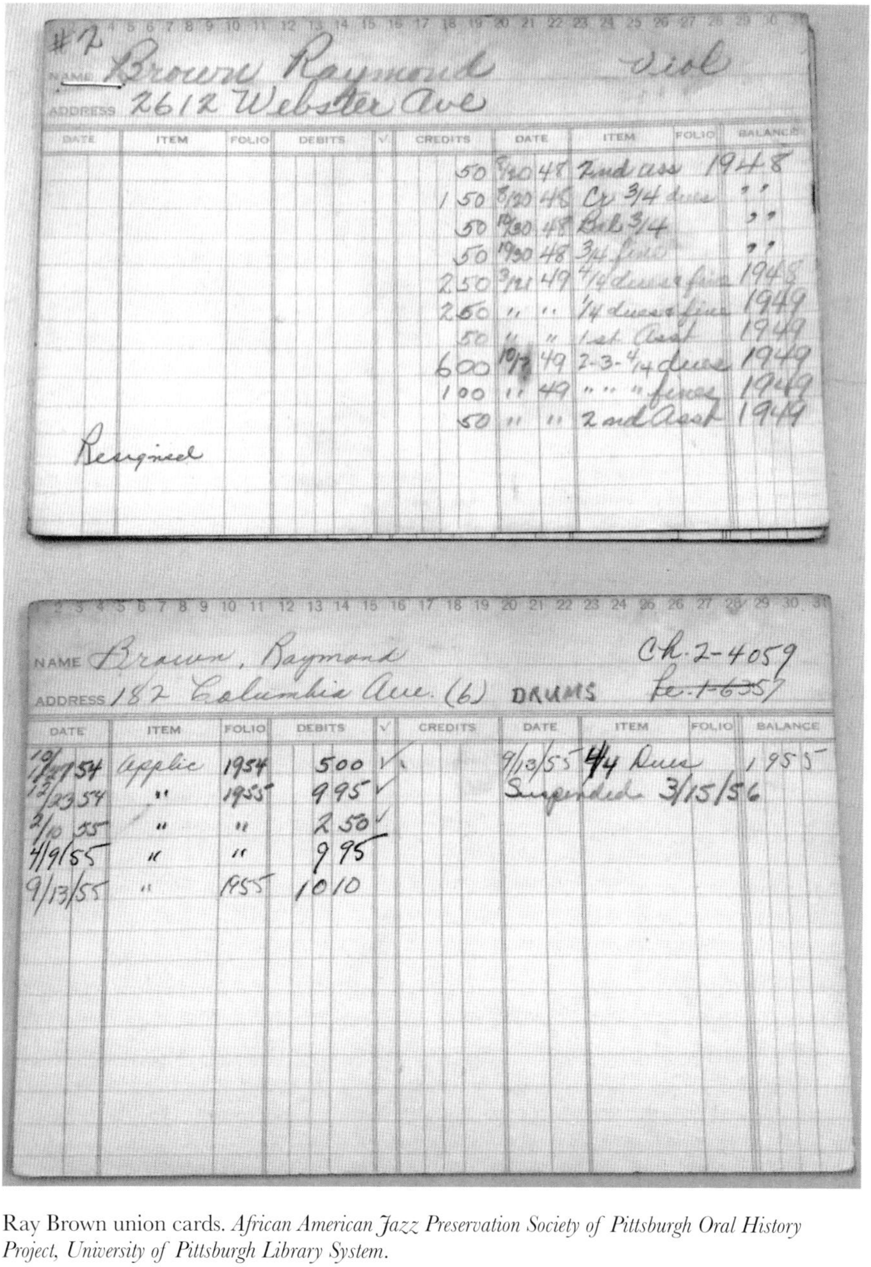

Ray Brown union cards. *African American Jazz Preservation Society of Pittsburgh Oral History Project, University of Pittsburgh Library System.*

Top: Al Aarons union card. Aaron was one of several Pittsburgh artists who played for the Count Basie Orchestra. *African American Jazz Preservation Society, of Pittsburgh Oral History Project, University of Pittsburgh Library System.*

Bottom: Art Nance union card. *African American Jazz Preservation Society of Pittsburgh Oral History Project, University of Pittsburgh Library System.*

Top: Roger Humphries union card. Humphries performed with Stanley Turrentine, Horace Silver, Ray Charles, Lionel Hampton, Coleman Hawkins, Dizzy Gillespie and Milt Jackson, among others. He still performs in the Pittsburgh area. *African American Jazz Preservation Society of Pittsburgh Oral History Project, University of Pittsburgh Library System.*

Bottom: Walt Harper union card. *African American Jazz Preservation Society of Pittsburgh Oral History Project, 1995–1999, University of Pittsburgh Library System.*

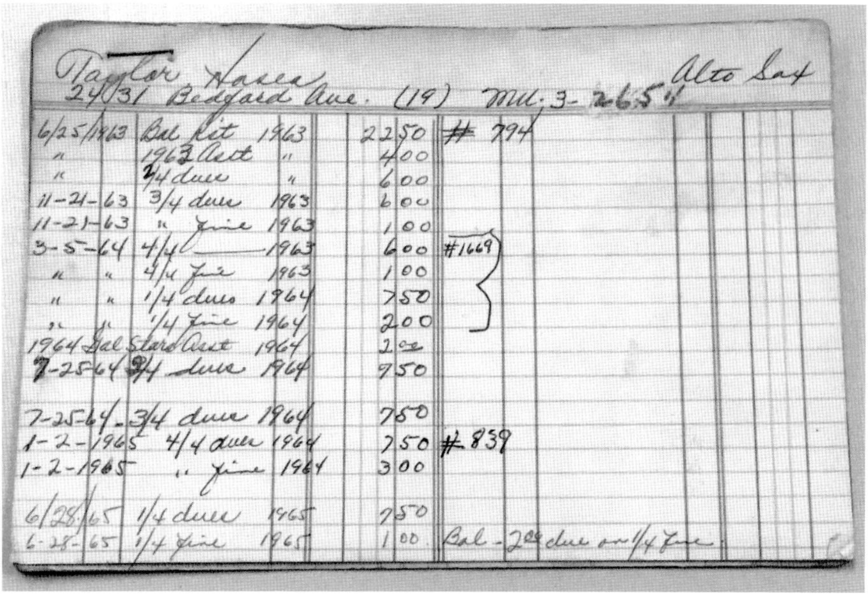

Hosea Taylor union card. *African American Jazz Preservation Society of Pittsburgh Oral History Project, Archives & Special Collections, University of Pittsburgh Library System.*

James Petrillo, the powerful president of the AFM, who ruled the music world from 1940 to 1958, resisted.

He opposed mergers and blocked efforts to prevent the merger of his own union, Local 10 in Chicago, with Local 208, which represented Black musicians. Petrillo's opposition to mergers led to his ouster as national president of the AFM. He later was forced to concede the time was coming when a nationwide merger of the white and Black locals in major cities would be forced on them. "You can't settle the race question in a minute but whether you like it or not, you are going to have to take in the colored boys," said Petrillo in an article in the *Pittsburgh Courier*. Ironically, Petrillo, after his retirement, led efforts as head of the federation's civil rights division to end segregation of union locals by traveling the North and South persuading white members to stand down in their opposition.

Austen, former president of the African American Jazz Preservation Society, thought the lawsuit would be a "no brainer." "All we had to do was show a history of employment discrimination." That was easy, Austin said in an oral history of the Jazz Preservation Society.

Segregation in Pittsburgh prevented Black musicians from performing in white-owned clubs that paid more than Black clubs. But when segregation ended nothing changed. When our unions merged, nothing changed. Yet we expected things to change. We expected a more level playing field…so we had to go to court to be heard. I must have been nuts thinking the strength of the case would prevail. We should have won. All we wanted was the back pay we would have earned if we had been allowed to perform after segregation was deemed unconstitutional. All we wanted was a little justice, a little dignity, a little respect.

11

THE WALLS CAME TUMBLING DOWN

The golden era of jazz ended in Pittsburgh on a May afternoon in 1956 as Pittsburgh mayor David Lawrence, wielding a crowbar adorned with a red ribbon, went through the motions of ripping off the doorframe of a ninety-year-old three-story Victorian house on Epiphany Street in the city's Lower Hill District.

Lawrence removed his fedora and donned a hardhat as a worker directed the mayor where to place the tool as newspaper photographers snapped pictures of the staged event. The house, with its arched windows and detailed woodwork, was the first of 976 buildings to be demolished, leaving the Lower Hill in rubble so the Civic Arena could be built. Another casualty of urban renewal was the demolition of approximately fifty clubs that had linked jazz to the Hill District since the 1920s.

The Crawford Grill, the Loendi Club, the Bambola, the Hurricane Lounge, the Musicians' Club and other nightspots were reduced to rubble and dust as the wrecking ball destroyed the history of the lower Hill District in the name of urban renewal, forcing the displacement of 1,800 Black and white families while creating new slums in other parts of the city and forever changing the jazz landscape.

Jack Robin, executive director of the Urban Redevelopment Authority, said the lower Hill District had to be destroyed in order to save it, but the transformation came at the expense of poor Black and white families who lived in the Hill District and were uprooted by the city's renewal project. It simply moved residents from one slum to another.

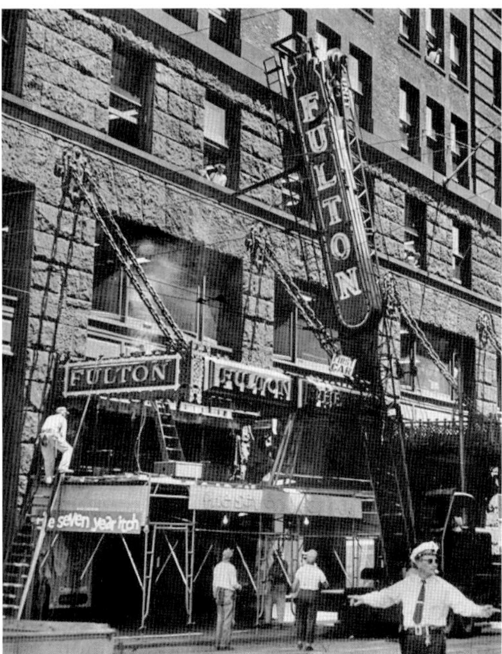

Above: Demolition of Lower Hill District was the ruination of jazz in Pittsburgh after a number of clubs were razed in the name of urban renewal. *University of Pittsburgh Library System.*

Left: Fulton Theater, twenty-five-year-old marquee being removed, July 1955. The Fulton opened as the Gayety in 1904 and was renamed Fulton in the 1930s. The theater was purchased in 1988 by the Pittsburgh Cultural Trust and was restored and reopened as Byham. *University of Pittsburgh Library System.*

View of Epiphany Church in the Hill District that was razed during urban renewal. Churches kept the African American community together and helped foster jazz. *Erroll Garner Archive, University of Pittsburgh Library System.*

The Hill had a thriving entertainment culture. Clubs in other parts of the city couldn't compete with the nightspots in the Hill District. "Downtown just didn't have it," said Chuck Austin, president of the African American Jazz Preservation Society of Pittsburgh. "When they built the arena, they killed jazz here."

Pianist Walt Harper said jazz was "exploding" in the 1950s and was popular among both Black and white audiences. Saxophonist Hosea Taylor, as a teenager, trolled the Hill District listening to jazz emanating from the dozens of clubs and bars. "I walked the back streets, narrow alley ways and visited all kinds of speakeasies and places that I didn't know existed let alone expected to actually be there," he told Kenan F. Foley in an interview for Kenan's 2007 dissertation, "The Interpretation of Experience. A Contextual Study of the Art of Three Pittsburgh Jazz Drummers."

East Liberty was another hotbed of jazz that suffered a similar fate. East Liberty was the third-busiest shopping area of the state behind downtown Pittsburgh and Philadelphia. It had forty-eight nightclubs and produced more than its share of jazz greats. Among them were Erroll Garner, Mary Lou Williams, Ahmad Jamal, Billy Strayhorn and Dodo Marmarosa. The neighborhood had more than five hundred businesses and a population of fourteen thousand. More than five thousand residents were displaced, and 230 acres were used to construct a highway to circle the neighborhood.

Above: Rooftop view of East Liberty, Centre Avenue—Sheridan Square Theater, Cameraphone Theater and Liberty Theater. *Pittsburgh City Photographer Collection, University of Pittsburgh Library System.*

Left: East Liberty All-Stars from left, Jerry Elliott, George Green, Nelson Harrison, Dodo Marmarosa and Danny Conn. *Courtesy of Nelson Harrison.*

Frank Cunimondo began playing piano in nightclubs and after-hours joints at thirteen. People left nightclubs when they closed and hit the after-hours spots to listen to jazz until daybreak. Urban renewal "absolutely ruined East Liberty," making it harder to navigate even for locals. "I was born in East Liberty and I can't find my way around East Liberty," Cunimondo said in an interview. "There were more nightclubs in Pittsburgh than you could shake a stick at. They were packed every night. I can't tell you how exciting it was to be a musician in those days."

The lifestyle took a toll on a musician's personal life. Cunimondo was married and divorced three times. Fellow musicians became heroin addicts or alcoholics. Personal relationships were difficult to maintain. After urban renewal reconfigured East Liberty, musicians had to scramble to find other work because they could not subsist on the earnings of being a musician.

East Liberty had been controlled by the Mafia for decades, according to a 1990 investigation by the now-defunct Pennsylvania Crime Commission. Ironically, it was the mob in East Liberty that kept jazz alive because they controlled places like the Bachelor's Club, the Del Moro Canoe Club, the Bocce Club and the Policemen's Club, where jazz musicians performed while gamblers shot craps and played barbut in a backroom hidden behind a thick curtain. Cunimondo rubbed elbows with some of Pittsburgh's most notorious hoodlums and the rough, violent men who frequented the after-hours clubs. "They were just mob guys to us. They never bothered us," he added. He recalled working at one club when the head of the Pittsburgh vice and narcotics squad came in with his prostitute girlfriend and got into a lovers' quarrel that ended with the girlfriend shooting the police officer. "I almost got killed. I was right next to him."

Cunimondo frequently played at the Almono, an after-hours club located behind the Allegheny County. Courthouse in Pittsburgh that was a hangout for politicians, cops, businessmen, hookers and racketeers. The club was dimly lit and had an ornate bar in the shape of a question mark—its ceiling lights were shaped like commas. The *Pittsburgh Press* reported in 1948 that "what significance the punctuation has is known only to bonafide members." He also worked at Club 30 for Frank Valenti, who was a suspect in two murders and later headed the mafia in Rochester, New York. "He was a nice guy," Cunimondo said.

Cunimondo started learning to play the tenor sax before making his reputation as a jazz pianist. At thirteen, he was playing sax and piano professionally. By seventeen, he was performing six nights a week at the Genovese Cocktail Lounge, a rough place owned by three brothers: Michael, Felix and Fiore Genovese. Michael Genovese later became head of La Cosa Nostra in Western Pennsylvania and was one of dozens of Mafia bosses nabbed during a raid at the infamous mob summit in Apalachin, New York, in 1957.

Cunimondo once played piano at the Executive Lounge, owned by mobster Anthony "Ninny the Torch" Lagattuta. When Cunimondo was hired, Lagattuta bought him a seven-foot-long Steinway piano that cost $100,000. When the club burned, investigators could not find any parts of the piano in the ashes. Cunimondo said Lagattuta told detectives he said the piano "out for a tune-up." Ninny was a convicted arsonist with a reputation that he could make cement burn. He had a bad habit of beating up his customers and once beat to death an attorney at his club, but he was acquitted.

Other clubs reduced to rubble during the demolition were the Aurora, the Java Jungle, Torch Club, J&J Bar, Five and Dime Bar and the Hilltop, which were popular places to listen to jazz. Men in tuxedos and women wearing long gowns flocked to the Harlem Casino on weekends in the 1930s. "I was too young to go in so I used to stand across the street and check it out," said vibes player DeRuyter "Ducky" Kemp in a 1982 article in the *Pittsburgh Post-Gazette*. "Ever hear some people say they were born 20 years too late. I really was."

The Savoy Ballroom located in the Pythian Temple attracted crowds of up to two thousand to hear Count Basie, Duke Ellington and Jimmie Lunceford perform. The Pythian Temple drew its audience from Western Pennsylvania, Ohio and West Virginia. Manager Sellers McKee Hall booked Jelly Roll Morton, McKinney's Detroit Cotton Pickers, Billy Paige's Broadway Syncopators and Lois Deppe and his Symphonian Syncopators.

Jazz, like scotch, is an acquired taste, and the city's musical tastes began to change. Other clubs tried to fill the musical gap, but attempts to keep the music alive were futile. Jazz was on life support as remaining clubs struggled to find an audience and music jobs were hard to come by. The city's white ruling class focused on saving the downtown and its property values. The men behind the drive to rebuild Pittsburgh were white; graduates of Harvard, Yale and Princeton; Republican; and Presbyterians and Episcopalians, wrote Roy Lubove in *Twentieth-Century Pittsburgh: Government, Business and Environmental Change, Volume 1.*

If Lawrence was the engine that drove the urban renewal project, millionaire Republican industrialist Richard King Mellon was "the sparkplug of the entire Renaissance," Lawrence said. "There is no part of Pittsburgh's Renaissance that will be greater than what we begin here today," reported the *Pittsburgh Press*.

Mellon didn't attend the ceremony that day, so his stand-in, Arthur Van Buskirk, vice president of the influential T. Mellon and Sons, called the development "a typical democratic process—no party, no race, no color, no creed," according to the *Pittsburgh Sun-Telegraph*.

When World War II ended, Pittsburgh focused its attention on a rebuilding plan that had been put on hold since 1941, when America went to war. City fathers recognized the need to reduce air pollution and control flooding, which wreaked havoc downtown. They also realized they had to clean up the discharges from the coal mines and steel mills that were ruining the Allegheny, Monongahela and Ohio Rivers.

The city had always been known among locals as "Smoketown." The New *York Daily Graphic* wrote in 1882 that "Pittsburgh is a place where the inhabitants breathe more and have their being in soot and grime; where the smoke is so dense that a cyclone would only scare the people by making the sun visible for a few minutes." In 1885, writer Willard Grazier wrote, "Pittsburg is a smoky, dismal city at her best," in *Peculiarities of American Cities.*

Lawrence, a Democrat, and Mellon, a Republican, forged an unlikely political alliance in the late 1940s to push forward a plan to transform Pittsburgh from a drab city into a shiny, modern metropolis. Pittsburgh was city exhausted from years of steel production during World War II. Buildings in the downtown area were blackened with soot from decades of pollution that stuck to the bricks like glue. Manufacturing plants, along with railroads, crisscrossed the city, and covering the air above Pittsburgh was a blanket of thick smog that forced motorists to turn on their headlights to see the road ahead. Train traffic added to the problem, coating the city with a blanket of thick smog that made it difficult to see in the daytime. The winter of 1947–48 became known as the "Black Snow Winter" after a thick layer of soot covered blanks of white snow.

Robert Pease, then director of the Allegheny Conference on Development, said in an interview contained in the Stanton Balfour Collection at the University of Pittsburgh that Lawrence believed if Pittsburgh were to survive as a major city, it "has to be a big-league city. We have to have major league ball teams, major league symphony, major league government: and to have to have a major league stadium and major league symphony halls."

Lawrence and Mellon delivered the death knell for jazz because they were focused on smoke and flood control, building new highways and revitalizing the downtown, not neighborhoods, wrote Roy Lubove in *Twentieth-Century Pittsburgh: The Post Steel Era.* "The Hill was Pittsburgh's Harlem," Lubove wrote.

Mellon and Lawrence didn't care about jazz or Black culture. What they cared about was removing an urban blight on the city. "Urban renewal" was simply a code word for "negro removal," charged Frank Bolden, then-editor of the *Pittsburgh Courier*, the city's influential Black weekly newspaper.

When ground was broken to construct the arena in 1958, the *Courier* noted the scarcity of Black officials or spectators at the groundbreaking. "Jim Crow Hovers Over Civic Arena," read the *Courier*'s headline. After the ceremony concluded, a work crew began the dismantling in earnest, leaving a cloud of dust and debris in their wake before moving onto the next building.

Newspaper photographs of the event clearly showed the separation between the white and Black residents present. Mayor Lawrence and other white officials were featured in the pictures while Black people standing in the crowd were treated as an afterthought, according to Dr. Laura

Grantmyre, whose doctoral dissertation, "Making the Implicit Explicit: Racial Biases in Urban Redevelopers' Images of Pittsburgh's Lower Hill District, 1947–1968." Hill District residents wanted to preserve their neighborhood, but city officials ignored their concerns and plowed ahead with redevelopment, turning the Lower Hill into a pile of rubble and broken memories.

White Pittsburgh had the Carnegie, Frick, Mellon and Heinz families, Black Pittsburgh had Strayhorn, Eldridge, Williams, Blakey and Eckstine. The renaissance was supported by financial and political heavy hitters who steamrolled the Black community and ignored their concerns. The *Pittsburgh Press* compared the renewal program to nuclear fission as "one project touched off another in chain-reaction fashion."

The only people who profited from the relocation were the absentee landlords who owned the rundown tenements. Landlords were paid exorbitant sums for their properties even though city assessors found that most were beyond repair or renovation. The owner of a rundown rooming house received $11,600 from the city even though he had refused past city orders to repair his decaying building.

The Hill District had been an eyesore for decades, a slum district filled with vice, unpaved streets and tenements that were unfit for human habitation. The *Pittsburgh Courier* reported that out of 1,691 buildings that were inspected by the city, 661 were in danger of collapsing. No one should live in them, but people still did. "Living conditions in the Hill District are neither desirable, acceptable nor endurable," said Jack Robin, head of the Urban Redevelopment Authority in a 1956 edition of the *Pittsburgh Press*.

Lawrence wanted to raze the Lower Hill so it could serve as a buffer for the downtown, where commercial property values were decreasing. The mayor and city planners envisioned a "cultural acropolis" in the Hill District above the Civic Arena that would contain two theaters, a home for the Pittsburgh Opera, an art museum and a hall for the Pittsburgh Symphony. The Culture District exists today downtown with the Pittsburgh Symphony Orchestra, the Civic Light Opera, the opera, the ballet, the Public Theater and the August Wilson African American Cultural Center.

By 1956, the *Pittsburgh Press* noted buildings on the lower Hill were boarded up with signs reading "Keep Out, Rat Poison." The streets were no longer jammed with shoppers, as residents scrambled to find other places to live. "You just don't uproot people no matter what kind of hovel they live in and replace them," the *Press* reported in an editorial.

Top: Aerial view of downtown Pittsburgh from Hill District. The Hill District served as a buffer for downtown. City officials were concerned about the Hill's effect on downtown commercial property values. *University of Pittsburgh Library System.*

Bottom: Wylie Avenue as seen from Tunnel Street in 1912. The Allegheny County Courthouse can be seen in the background. *University of Pittsburgh Library System.*

The Civic Arena was the centerpiece of Hill District redevelopment, an idea conceived by councilman Abraham Wolk and department store magnate Edgar Kaufmann, who wanted a home for their beloved Civic Light Opera, but the project came with a price beyond the millions of dollars of public and private money that eventually was pumped into it. Initially, the site was to be called the Lower Hill Cultural Center, but the name was quickly changed to the Civic Arena. City planners envisioned audiences listening to Mozart, Puccini or Verdi beneath a dark, star-filled summer sky under a retractable roof. Kaufmann publicly displayed a working model of the arena at a meeting of the Urban Redevelopment Authority, pledged $1.5 million toward its construction and convinced other corporate leaders to contribute another $2.5 million.

The CLO was created in 1946 and staged its productions at Pitt Stadium in the city's Oakland neighborhood, where the University of Pittsburgh was located. Sometimes the productions in the early years had to be canceled because of rain, and questions were raised whether the opera could become a cultural fixture in the city without a permanent home.

Wolk decided the opera company needed a home that was immune to weather. Kaufmann exhibited a scale model of the arena to reporters and demonstrated how the roof retracted. After the arena opened, the roof failed to work regularly and later was closed permanently. Instead of operas and musicals, the building was used for sporting events and as a backdrop for Hollywood movies and jazz concerts featuring Art Blakey and Walt Harper of Pittsburgh along with nationally known artists such as Duke Ellington, Elvis Presley, Frank Sinatra, the Rolling Stones, Michael Jackson, the Beatles and Britney Spears until it was demolished and replaced by the PPG Paints Arena, the home of the Pittsburgh Penguins.

The lower Hill District was demolished with little thought to the feelings of Black residents and small business owners who lost their property through eminent domain. The massive urban renewal project ended a glamorous but short-lived Black renaissance in Pittsburgh. City newspapers praised the construction of the Civic Arena as a civic asset. Even the Black community initially praised the plan. The *Pittsburgh Courier* predicted in 1977 that by 2000, the lower Hill District would be part of an industrial and residential complex linking the Hill to the downtown. That prediction never came true. "The men of the Renaissance have been unable to produce anything but a crop of weeds on 9.2 acres of prime public land next to the Civic Arena," the *Pittsburgh Press* wrote in 1961.

When demolition crews began bulldozing structures, the streets of the Lower Hill emptied, and business owners and landlords boarded up their buildings amid the dust, rubble and rats that soon occupied the vacant structures, according to the *Pittsburgh Press*. Displaced residents wondered where they would live, and jazz musicians wondered if they would be able to find work since many of their musical haunts were razed.

Resistance among the Black community surfaced. Community activists erected a billboard with a warning to city officials not to consider further redevelopment past a certain point. By 1967, residents realized they had been hoodwinked, and most of the promises were never fulfilled.

Historian Lewis Mumford visited Pittsburgh and walked through the Lower Hill during the summer of 1957 with Robert Pease, looking at the old brick houses and trying to decide if any could be saved. When the tour was over, Mumford turned to Pease and said, "You know, I don't see any redeeming grace; I don't see anything that is worth saving," reported the *Pittsburgh Press*.

12

THE GREATS

Billy Strayhorn

Young Dr. Kildare, starring Lew Ayres and Lionel Barrymore, was the feature film playing at the Stanley Theater in Pittsburgh on December 2, 1938. Billy Strayhorn was more interested in music than movies on that cold day. The twenty-three-year-old Strayhorn was there to meet Duke Ellington, whose orchestra was the performing. Strayhorn and a friend, George Greenlee, waited outside the theater with quarters in hand to listen to Ellington's orchestra perform and then meet the bandleader backstage.

Ellington had invited Strayhorn, whom he had yet to meet, to his dressing room to audition for a job with his orchestra by playing his version of one of Ellington's compositions. A day earlier, George Greenlee met Ellington in the inner sanctum of the Crawford Grill, where his uncle Gus Greenlee, the noted jazz promoter, racketeer and sportsman, was holding court. Greenlee introduced his nephew to Ellington and told him about a talented young man Ellington should meet. Stop by the theater the next day, Ellington told George, and bring your friend.

Ellington sat in his dressing room with his eyes closed while his valet conked his hair as Strayhorn was ushered in to see him. He invited Strayhorn to sit down at the piano in his dressing room and play his arrangement of "Something to Live For." Ellington was impressed and gave Strayhorn several assignments during the orchestra's engagement at the Stanley. To

Stanley Theater on Seventh Street looking toward Liberty Avenue. *University of Pittsburgh Library System.*

Strayhorn's surprise, Ellington's band performed Strayhorn's arrangement of "Two Sleepy People." Ellington offered Strayhorn a job, but it would be several weeks before Strayhorn arrived in Harlem on the "'A' Train" with the directions Ellington had provided.

Strayhorn had been studying classical piano when he heard Ellington's orchestra on the radio in 1934. "I was hooked. I went and stood right in front, right on the piano all evening," wrote the *New York Times* in Strayhorn's 1967 obituary. "He played everything and I was lost. I didn't have anything to say and I just stood there with my mouth open."

Billy Strayhorn had gone from being a soda jerk and delivery boy at a Pittsburgh drugstore to arranger, composer and alter ego for Ellington, a complex relationship that lasted nearly thirty years. The diminutive Strayhorn, whose nickname was "Peanut," was the musical force behind some of Ellington's greatest works, "Take the 'A' Train," "Satin Doll" and "Lush Life," but Strayhorn didn't always receive full credit for his musical contributions. Strayhorn didn't seem to mind. "I function independently," Strayhorn told *New York Times* music critic John S Wilson in 1965. "He is he. I am me. He has never made me feel that I am walking in his shadow."

Billy Strayhorn met Duke Ellington through jazz promoter Gus Greenlee. *Library of Congress.*

Strayhorn wrote "Take the 'A' Train" based on the directions Ellington gave him in Pittsburgh so he could find Ellington's apartment in the Sugar Hill section of Harlem. In 1939, the year the song was written, the A line in New York City's subway system ran from Brooklyn to Harlem and Manhattan. The song became the signature tune for Ellington's orchestra, replacing "Sepia Panorama" that Ellington had been using.

Ellington's son, Mercer, found the composition for "Take the 'A' Train" in the trash and retrieved it after Strayhorn had discarded the work because he thought the song sounded too much like a Fletcher Henderson piece, according to Stuart Nicholson's *Reminiscing in Tempo—A Portrait of Duke Ellington.*

Wilson explained the musical partnership between the two men when Ellington once called him early one morning in 1958 while Strayhorn was still asleep. "We are writing this suite," Ellington told him. "We are?" Strayhorn replied. "I need three or four minutes in D flat. Do it."

The discussion was over. Strayhorn had barely finished the work for the Great South Bay Jazz Festival when the song was handed out to the musicians, who performed it without rehearsing. Strayhorn was a sickly child after he was born. His parents weren't sure what to name him, and he was in the fifth grade before his parents legally named him William Thomas Strayhorn. His family moved around the Pittsburgh area to Braddock and Rankin before settling in Homewood, a racially mixed neighborhood. As his musical skills grew, he began playing piano at cocktail parties and entertaining customers at the pharmacy where he worked and whenever he made deliveries to their homes if they happened to have a piano.

He wrote a ten-song production, *Fantastic Rhythm*, while still in high school, and it was performed at several other city high schools as well as at other venues in suburban towns. He studied music under the tutelage of Carl McVicker at Westinghouse High School. McVicker once heard Strayhorn play Edvard Grieg's *Piano Concerto in A Minor, op. 16* in 1934 and recognized Strayhorn's immense talent. "I never heard a student play that way or after," McVicker told Strayhorn biographer David Hadju in *Lush Life.* "The orchestra may have been a group of students but Billy Strayhorn was a professional artist."

Another music teacher who influenced Strayhorn was Jane Alexander. "If any one teacher is to be credited with influencing young Pittsburghers' love of music, and their ability to express themselves through it, Mrs. Alexander must be prominently mentioned," said Strayhorn in a 1960 article in the *Pittsburgh Press.*

"She did a wonderful thing for me: she taught me a basic progression, and I did that for two years. Couldn't vary. Had to do it in all kinds of ways. Of course, I hated it. But it was invaluable training," he said in a 1962 interview contained in the archives of the H. John Heinz History Center in Pittsburgh.

After high school, his first professional job came performing at Charlie Ray's, an East Liberty after-hours club owned by an ex-boxer. He later played at the Apple Club run by numbers kingpin Woogie Harris, Gus Greenlee's partner in the gambling rackets.

Strayhorn was a heavy smoker and liked to drink. He developed esophageal cancer and underwent radiation in 1966. His last composition for Ellington was "Blood Count," a song based on his cancer treatment. Strayhorn died in 1967. He was fifty-one.

Earl "Fatha" Hines

Ragtime pianist Eubie Blake had some advice for fellow pianist Earl Hines after hearing him play at a Pittsburgh club. Get out of Pittsburgh, Blake said, because Hines had too much talent to remain a musician in the city. He told Hines's aunt Sadie Phillips, "This boy's a genius. He has no business staying here," according to *A Natural History of the Piano* by Stuart Isacoff. Blake delivered a much sterner admonition to Hines directly.

"If I catch you here again, I'm going to take that cane and wrap it out all over your head if you're not gone when I come back. Do you realize you can stay here in Pittsburgh the rest of your life and still be the same boy you are now? You got to get away from here."

Hines's life was surrounded by music. He was born in Duquesne in a twelve-room house that included his father, stepmother, grandparents, two cousins, two uncles and an aunt. His father played the trumpet, his mother the piano. His father also led the Eureka Brass Band, which played at picnics and other events around Pittsburgh.

Hines took lessons from Emma D. Young and, later, a German teacher, Von Holz, who taught classical music. "I studied to be a classical pianist and placed all my heart and soul to be a concert master but we had racial trouble as to be a black man in that type of music," said Hines, according to a doctoral dissertation by Jeff Farley, "Making America's Music: Jazz History and the Jazz Preservation Act," at the University of Glasgow. Hines was influenced musically by stride pianists Luckey Roberts and James P.

Robinson, who developed the technique of using their right hands to play the melody of a tune while using their left hands to alternate between a single note and chords.

"Far more than any other musician, Hines stands out as responsible for pushing jazz piano beyond the limiting horizontal structure of ragtime and into the versatile linear approach, one that continues to hold sway to this day," wrote jazz historian Ted Gioia in *The History of Jazz*.

When Hines was seventeen, he began playing piano at the Leader House with Lois Deppe and his Symphony Serenaders for fifteen dollars a week. Deppe was born in Horse Cave, Kentucky, and raised in Ohio but was recognized as a Pittsburgh talent who started the first Black swing band in the city. In 1921, Hines formed a trio with violinist Emmett Jordan and drummer Harry Williams. Three years later, Hines formed another band with Benny Carter on sax and Cuban Bennett on drums.

In 1925, Deppe moved to Chicago. Hines, in his late teens, soon followed, and he made a name for himself playing at the Elite Club, Regal Theatre, the Apex Club, the Sunset Café, the Savoy Ballroom and the Grand Terrace. which was owned by mobster Al Capone. In a British documentary made for ATV Television, *Earl "Fatha" Hines*, made in 1975, Hines recalls the night Capone came to the club and set down the rules for the band:

> *Al came in there one night and called the whole band and show together and said, "Now we want to let you know our position. We just want you people just to attend to your own business. We'll give you all the Protection in the world but we want you to be like the three monkeys: you hear nothing and you see nothing and you say nothing." And that's what we did. And I used to hear many of the things that they were going to do but I never did tell anyone. Sometimes the Police used to come in…looking for a fall guy and say, "Earl what were they talking about?"…But I said, "I don't know—no, you're not going to pin that on me," because they had a habit of putting the pictures of different people that would bring information in the newspaper and the next day you would find them out there in the lake somewhere swimming around with some chains attached to their feet if you know what I mean.*

In 1928, Hines recorded a series of songs with Louis Armstrong that became "Weather Bird," "one of the most important, and fruitful, and influential collaborations in American music," wrote Jeffrey Taylor in the *Musical Quarterly* in 1998.

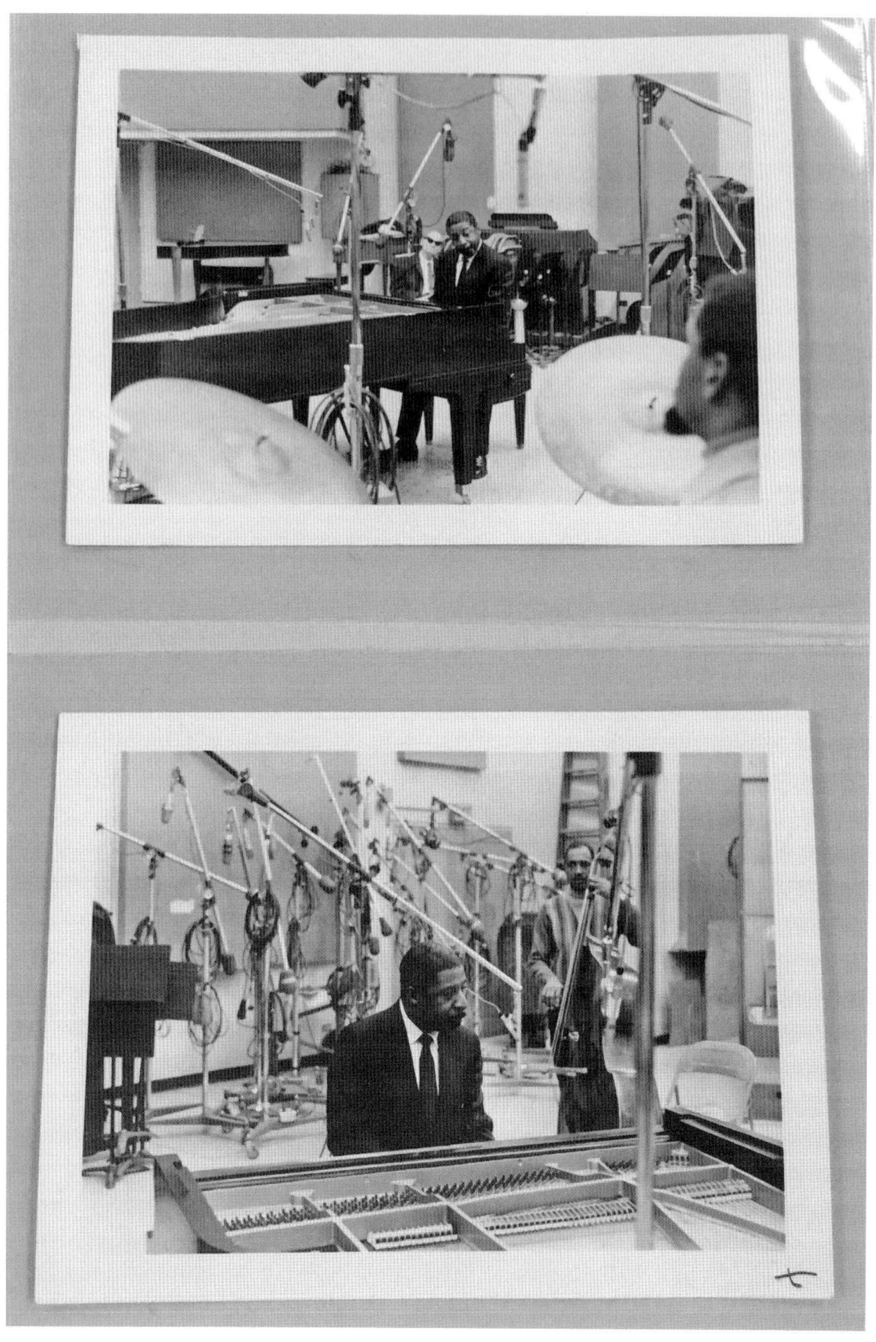

Erroll Garner performs in the studio. *Erroll Garner Archive, University of Pittsburgh Library System.*

Hines loved clothes and always traveled with three trunks of clothes. He didn't buy expensive suits but ones that looked good and fit well. He owned several so he could change them frequently without wearing them out. He bought his custom-made shoes from the Chicago Theatrical Shoe store, according to an interview in *American Musicians: Fifty-Six Portraits in Jazz* by Whitney Balliett. If Hines needed a new pair while on tour, the store had his measurements on hand and could send him a new pair wherever he was performing.

Hines played what critics called "trumpet style" piano by playing horn-like solo lines in octaves with his right hand and spurring them with chords from his left. "He thus carved a place for the piano as a solo instrument outside the rhythm section and defined the roles of both hands for the next generations of jazz pianists," wrote Jon Pareles, a music critic for the *New York Times* in 1983 when Hines died.

ERROLL GARNER

Erroll Garner was known as "the man with forty fingers" and had the fastest left hand in music. He was ambidextrous and signed autographs with both hands simultaneously. Garner played the piano by ear. He could not read music but could repeat songs flawlessly. He recorded twenty songs in an afternoon with a broken index finger. "His left hand played like it belong to another person," reported the *New York Times*.

Garner was barred from joining Local 471 of the Musicians Union in Pittsburgh because he could not read music, although he later was made an honorary member. Garner sometimes bristled when asked about his failure to learn to read music. "Does a beaver have to have an engineering degree to build a dam?" he once responded to an interviewer's question in an article contained in the Garner archives at the University of Pittsburgh. "You're paid to play notes, not read them."

Nelson Harrison said he once interviewed Garner on public television in Pittsburgh, and Garner told Harrison that he had spent a year studying at Juilliard. "What really happened was they were studying him," Harrison said in an interview. "Would you ask Stevie Wonder if he could read music? Would you ask Ray Charles if he could read music?"

Garner's *Concert by the Sea*, performed in an old church in Carmel-by-the-Sea in 1955, is considered by critics to be the best piano jazz concert

Left: Erroll Garner when he was with the Jazz Messengers. *Erroll Garner Archive, Archives & Special Collections, University of Pittsburgh Library System.*

Below: Erroll Garner at the piano in 1963. People always asked about his inability to read sheet music. Garner would respond, "Does a beaver have to have an engineering degree to build a dam?" *Erroll Garner Archive, University of Pittsburgh Library System.*

Erroll Garner in classroom. *Erroll Garner Archive, University of Pittsburgh Library System.*

of all time. The concert was recorded with Denzil Best on drums and Eddie Cochran on bass. Garner sweat so much that he went through four sets of clothing because he was drenched to the skin. The liner notes on the album call the work "the product for what jazz piano and jazz concert albums must be."

A soldier stationed at Fort Ord in California taped the concert on a reel-to-reel recorder to entertain his fellow soldiers. Garner's agent, Martha Glaser, asked the soldier for the tape, promising to him "copies of every record Erroll ever made but I can't let you keep that tape," according to the Erroll Garner Papers at the University of Pittsburgh. Martha Glaser gave the tape to George Avakian of Columbia Records, who immediately recorded the album. Lyricist Johnny Burke wrote the words to the song made popular by Johnny Mathias and sold 2.5 million copies.

Garner was inspired to write his signature song, "Misty," during a rainy flight from San Francisco to Denver when he looked out the window and he saw a rainbow through the midst. "I wrote 'Misty' from a beautiful rainbow I saw when I was flying from a stop off in Denver. This rainbow was fascinating because it wasn't long but very wide and in every color you

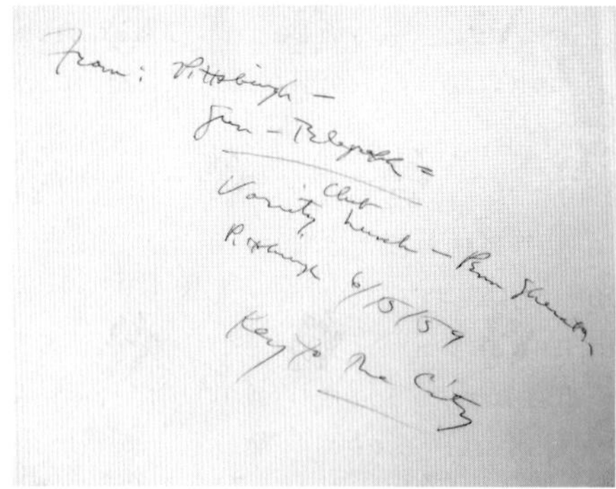

Left: Hand-written note about receiving "Key to the City" in Pittsburgh in 1959. *Erroll Garner Archive, University of Pittsburgh Library System.*

Below: Garner usually traveled with the Manhattan telephone directory to sit on because he was short. He once forgot it when traveling and had to round up local phone books to sit on. *Erroll Garner Archive, University of Pittsburgh Library System.*

can imagine. With the dew drops and the windows being misty, that fine rain, that's how I named it 'Misty'," he recalled in Whitney Balliett's *American Musicians: Fifty-Six Portraits in Jazz*.

Garner dropped to his knees in the aisle of the plane, pretending he had a piano and grunting as he composed. An older woman sitting next to him thought he was having a medical emergency. "Where she is now, I don't know but I must say she was the first in on 'Misty'."

In a 1959 profile, the New York Times noted that "he gets ideas, he says, from everything. A big color, the sound of water and wind, or a flash of something cool." Garner had a habit of grunting and stomping his feet with such vigor while he was playing that one Pittsburgh club owner placed a carpet beneath his feet to muffle the noise so it wouldn't detract from his performance, according to a 1967 article in *Down Beat* contained in Garner's papers at the University of Pittsburgh.

When he was in school, he was a member of an exclusive musical group known as the Kandy Kids that performed on radio. The group got its name because the station always had a bowl of candy at the ready during broadcasts. Garner's nickname was "Gumdrops," his favorite candy.

Garner was a short man, five feet, two inches tall, and had to sit on a Manhattan telephone directory so he could reach the keys. He once forgot the phone book and scrounged ten directories from the city where he was performing, piling them onto the stool.

Garner died in 1977, and his body was returned to Pittsburgh. As people entered the St. James AME Church in East Liberty on a sunny, snowy day, pianist George Duke Spaulding played a medley of Garner's compositions. As the church emptied, Spaulding played "Misty," according to the funeral program contained in the Garner archives at the University of Pittsburgh. In his eulogy, Reverend Alexander told mourners that Garner was not dead, just asleep. "He's just sleeping until the storm blows over. Then he will awake and things no longer will be misty."

ART BLAKEY

Art Blakey was a rebel and a survivor. He was a rulebreaker who was kicked out of school because he wouldn't conform. He began his musical career on the piano until he was forced to learn how to play drums. "I came into music as a matter of survival. I had to survive. I'm a depression baby and therefore

I didn't have much education," said Blakey in an interview with the Howard University Oral History Project.

> *I left school because I rebelled against what the schools were teaching...and the Board of Education found that it was best for me to get out of there. There wasn't room enough for me there and the principal at the junior high school I was in because I didn't go along with the teachers and what they taught about Africa and "Little Black Sambo." Therefore, I was barred from going to school so I went to work.*

Blakey was playing piano at a club in 1937 when fourteen-year-old Erroll Garner was in the audience. Blakey was struggling with the song when Garner stood up and said, "I can play that," according to a 1977 *Pittsburgh Press* story. Garner sat down at the piano and played the number flawlessly. After that, the club owner ordered Blakey to play the drums, an instrument Blakey had never played before. "We had a big argument. He said, 'you big dummy. You get up there and play the drums.' So, I went up there and played the drums and I've been playing them ever since. It wasn't a question of taking no lessons because there were no lessons to take. So, I just went up there and played the show (on drums)," Blakey recalled in an interview with the Percussive Arts Society when he was inducted into its Hall of Fame.

> *How, I'll never know, but I made it. I used to play every night. It didn't matter how much money I was making, I just had to play every night. When we'd get through playing at night, it was daybreak. Then we'd play the breakfast show. After that we'd have a jam session, which would go on until like 2:00 in the afternoon. So maybe by 3:00 I'd get to bed, and I'd be back in the club again at 8:30. So I never stopped. I was playing all the time, so I didn't have to worry about practicing.*

Blakey was the product of a shotgun marriage. Shortly after his parents were married, his father, Bertram Blakey, stopped at a drugstore, walked inside and then fled through a back door. He never saw his pregnant wife again until the day she died. "I was passing my father every day on the street without knowing it was my father," he said an interview at the Howard University Jazz Oral History Project.

When he was fifteen, Blakey became a father and husband after marrying his pregnant girlfriend. Together they lived in a $1.50-a-week room above a brothel. "Art was an original. He's the only drummer whose time I recognize immediately. And his signature style was amazing; we used to call him 'Thunder.' When I first met him on 52nd Street in 1944, he already had the polyrhythmic thing down," said Max Roach in Blakey's obituary in the *New York Times*. "Art was perhaps the best at maintaining independence with all four limbs. He was doing it before anybody was."

In Pittsburgh, Blakey played piano at clubs, performing off-color songs while moving the piano from table to table, according to a story in *Jazz Anecdotes: Second Time Around.* Blakey described the songs as "just filth," but the audiences loved it and he'd earn up to forty dollars a night in tips.

Blakey left Pittsburgh in 1942 for New York City, where he joined a band that Mary Lou Williams was forming. Two years later, he joined Fletcher Henderson's orchestra before hooking up with Billy Eckstine's band. He formed the Jazz Messengers in 1954 with Horace Silver, Hank Mobley and Kenny Dorham. The group nurtured such stars such as Branford and Wynton Marsalis, Benny Golsen, Wayne Shorter, Chuck Mangione and Slide Hampton. The Jazz Messengers disbanded upon Blakey's death in 1990 after producing classic albums *A Night in Tunisia* and *Moanin'*.

Blakey studied drumming in Africa in 1948 and adopted the Muslim name Abdullah Ibn Buhainam, though he rejected efforts by critics to link jazz to African culture. "Since so many of the great jazz musicians are Black, they try to connect us to Africa," he said. "But I'm an American Black man. We ain't got no connection to Africa. I imagine some of my people come from Africa, but there are some Irish people in there, too. I'm a human being and it don't make no difference where I come from. And they're trying to put [jazz] off in the corner as being Black," he added. "Jazz is American; it ain't got a damn thing to do with color. I'll take kids from any part of the world; if they want to play jazz, I'll put them in my band and they'll play jazz—and really play it, too."

Toward the end of his life, Blakey's hearing began to worsen. "The only thing I can hear is music," he said. "I can hear vibrations. I take my hearing aid off when I'm on the bandstand, and I can hear better than the other musicians; I know when they're out of tune."

MARY LOU WILLIAMS

Mary Lou Williams had perfect pitch and a good memory. She was playing hopscotch outside her home in the East Liberty area of Pittsburgh when Buzzin' Harris, a comedian and leader of a vaudeville tent show, asked her

Mary Lou Williams was from the East Liberty area of Pittsburgh and became known as the "little piano girl" performing for some of the city's wealthiest families. *Library of Congress.*

if she could play the piano after his pianist got drunk and failed to show up for a performance.

Williams had been recommended to Harris who thought someone was playing a joke on him when he saw that Williams was just a child. Could she read music? Harris asked. Williams astounded Harris by memorizing and playing the entire show's songs. He hired Williams, who spent two months in the summer of 1922 traveling to Detroit, Chicago, Cincinnati and St. Louis with Harris, performing in his show *Hits and Bits*.

Williams was born Mary Alfrieda Mae Scruggs in Atlanta, Georgia, in 1910, the illegitimate daughter of a father she didn't meet until four decades later and her mother, Virginia, who played the piano. Her mother married her stepfather, Fletcher Burley. Williams said loved her as if she was his own daughter, shared in an interview with Howard University's oral history project. "He loved me so much." She became Mary Lou Williams after marrying John "Bearcat" Williams.

Williams arrived in Pittsburgh at the age of four, and her family settled in East Liberty. The influx of Black migrants during the Great Migration created a housing shortage. People in East Liberty without a place to stay paid a nickel a night to sleep in boxcars with holes cut in the sides to let air in. Williams sat on her mother's lap when she was three while her mother played the piano and then repeated what her astounded mother had just played. "I didn't know what I was doing," she later recalled. She knew from the first time she started playing the piano that she would be a jazz performer and not a classical pianist.

When she was a student at Westinghouse High School, Williams discovered she had perfect pitch, according to a 1954 interview in *Melody Maker* magazine. "One day I pinch-hit for a tuning fork the teacher had lost, and it was discovered I possessed perfect pitch. Because this oddity spread throughout the school, pupils would drop pots, pans and other loud objects, asking 'What note Mary?'"

She developed a reputation as a pianist and began entertaining at the homes of East Liberty's elite, who sent their chauffeurs to pick her up. "I played for the Mellons. I became the 'little piano girl of East Liberty.'" A chauffeur would arrive at Williams's home to take her to a party and then return her home when she was done.

She also played for her stepfather, grandfather and uncle, who loved jazz and paid her fifty cents to hear their favorite songs. She listened to the records of Fats Waller, James Johnson, Willie "The Lion" Smith and Jelly Roll Morton. "I knew that I loved jazz," she said.

Fletcher Burley was a gambler and considered a rough customer because of his volatile temper, but he doted on Williams, she said. He took Williams to one of his gambling haunts wearing an oversize coat under which he used to hide Williams. Inside the club, a group of men sat around a table playing a card game known as Georgia skin. A piano sat along the wall. Williams played a few tunes, and Burley took off his hat, put a dollar inside and then passed the hat around the room, ordering his gambling cronies to each contribute. Williams earned as much as twenty dollars, but once outside, Burley demanded that she return his dollar contribution.

Burley was one of three men who were the most important in her life and recognized her talent. The others were Roland Mayfield, known as the "Black Prince of East Liberty," and Jack Howard. Williams described Mayfield as laconic man who was rich and smoked big cigars. He provided Williams whatever she needed. He bought her clothes and provided transportation to and from engagements. Jack Howard was a musical mentor who taught Williams piano techniques and how to use her left hand when playing to produce a larger sound with bass notes.

As she got older, Williams played at jam sessions at clubs from East Liberty to the Hill District. "We always wound up in the Subway on Wylie Avenue, a hole in the ground to which the cream of the crop came to enjoy the finest in entertainment. For me, it was paradise," she said in an interview with the Jazz Institute at Rutgers University.

On Saturday nights, Williams and her teenage friends would head for a theater that featured Black musical acts, where she focused on a female pianist who sat cross-legged in front of the piano with a cigarette dangling from her mouth. "I told myself, Mary, you'll do that one day," she told *Melody Maker* magazine in 1954.

Her reputation as a musician soon reached the jazz world in New York City even though she was only fifteen. "I was playing style of piano that was amazing to them. It was nothing to me." In the mid-1930s, she joined

Andy Kirk's Twelve Clouds of Joy. By seventeen, she was playing for Duke Ellington. She was back in Pittsburgh by 1942 and formed an ensemble that included Pittsburgher Art Blakey.

Three years later, she composed "Zodiac Suite," a complex piece of a dozen songs each for a sign of Zodiac and dedicated the songs to fellow musicians such as Billie Holiday, Duke Ellington and Bud Powell. Then, in 1954, Williams's behavior took a strange turn. She walked off the stage in mid-performance at the Boeuf sur le Toit in Paris—just closed the keyboard and walked off, vanishing for three years. "I really didn't stop on my own," she recalled in the Rutgers interview. "I just, so something carried me away and I never really thought about playing anymore."

She credited two Catholic priests, Father John Crowley and Father Anthony Woods, with convincing her to return to playing. When she resurfaced, she was a convert to Catholicism and later wrote highly spiritual works "Mary Lou's Mass," "Music for Peace" and "Black Christ of the Andes." She said jazz is a way of healing the soul. "It should be played everywhere—in churches, nightclubs, everywhere. We have to use every place we can," she told the *New York Post* in 1975.

Williams returned to Pittsburgh for burial after her death. The headline in the *Pittsburgh Courier* on June 1, 1981, was simple. "Mary Lou Williams Buried in Pittsburgh."

Klook Clarke

Drummer Kenny "Klook" Clarke spent part of his painful youth living at the Coleman Industrial School for Negro Boys in the Hill District with thirty-three other boys in a two-story house. His name at the time was Charles Clarke Spearman. He and his brother, Frank, a bassist, were placed in the school after their mother, Martha Grace Scott, died and their father, Charles Spearman, abandoned them. A stepfather, a Baptist preacher, refused to care for them, so he put in the orphanage.

The school was founded in 1907 by Samuel and Luella Coleman for homeless children. Clarke learned to play the drums while at Coleman. After living with a foster family, Clarke was on his own and lived in a room above a soda fountain. He began playing at Hill District clubs like Derby Dan's in the Hill District and at the Club Mirador in Homestead and landed his first professional job as a member of LeRoy Bradley's Band. He left Pittsburgh for New York City in 1935 when he was twenty-one.

He was drafted into the army in 1943 but went AWOL and landed a job with Cootie Williams's band until he was arrested and returned to the army and sent to Europe. In 1944, he married jazz singer Carmen McRae and converted to Islam and becoming Liaquat Ali Salaam. After his discharge, he joined Dizzy Gillespie's orchestra, where he developed his nickname, "Klook." Gillespie recorded "Oop Bop Sh'bam" and the scat lyrics in the song "Oop Bop Sh'bam a Klook Mop" became his moniker.

Clarke, one of the developers of bebop, developed a drumming technique that allowed him to use his right hand to play continuously on the top cymbal, known as the ride, while using his left hand to make dramatic, spontaneous sounds on the snare drum. Clarke performed with the top artists of his time. He worked with Miles Davis, Charles Mingus, Thelonious Monk, Dexter Gordon, Milt Jackson, Art Tatum, Charlie Parker, Louis Armstrong, Duke Ellington, Count Basie and Fats Navarro, among others. He became a founding member of the Modern Jazz Quartet and later, disgusted with racial discrimination in America, moved to Paris, where he spent thirty-one years.

He returned to Pittsburgh briefly to teach at the University of Pittsburgh at the request of his friend Dr. Nathan Davis, who headed the jazz studies department.

"It (racism) made me want to leave America," he said in an oral interview with the Rutgers University Institute for Jazz Studies. "It seemed like Alice in Wonderland to me. Europeans appreciated jazz more than American audiences. That's what impressed me so much."

Little Georgie Benson

Guitarist George Benson grew up in Pittsburgh's Hill District, living in a hotel owned by his grandfather, a man named Major Evans whose claim to fame was that he was able to lift the rear end of a car by himself. The hotel was located in an alley lined with dirty brick walls and a street filled with trash and rats.

His mother, Erma, was fifteen when Benson was born. His father, Charles, was serving in Europe during World War II. The Hill of Benson's youth was filled with street vendors selling ice and coal. The refrains of "ice man" and "coal man" echoed through the streets. Little Georgie sold newspapers near Stanley's Bar and Grille, one of many jazz joints in the Hill District, where Charlie Parker, Billy Eckstine and Art Blakey performed at times.

George Benson at Club Café on Pittsburgh's Southside. *Courtesy of Nelson Harrison.*

With the few cents he earned from selling papers, Benson and a cousin headed for Goode's Drug Store to buy candy, and one day, a customer asked Benson to sing. Benson sang "Blood Shot Eyes" by Wynonie Harris, and the man was so impressed that he tipped Benson, according to Benson's 2014 autobiography, *George Benson: The Autobiography.*

Benson remembered Pittsburgh as a city of steel mills, dust, ghettos, segregation and racism, but his ties ran deep. He recalled the noise of the mills, the dust-red sky at night and the sounds of music emanating from jukeboxes down the street. "When I die that's where I want to go. Put me under some of that coal dust," he told the *Pittsburgh Press* in 1985.

He started his musical career playing the ukulele for pennies on street corners when he was seven and then switched to the guitar when he was nine. He was known to residents as "Little Georgie Benson" and recorded his first song when he was ten.

Benson constructed a guitar out of cigar boxes. His stepfather, Thomas Collier, played the guitar and was a fan of guitarist Charlie Christian, a pioneer in the development of the electric guitar who played with the Benny Goodman Sextet. Collier retrieved his guitar from a pawn shop and warned his stepson not to touch the instrument, but Benson couldn't resist. "Now, you're going to have to learn to play it," Collier replied. "If you're going to be touching my guitar, you're going to have to learn how to play," Benson recalled in an interview recorded by the Smithsonian.

Collier turned on the amplifier. "He took the guitar and strummed it, brrrrmmm, and the sound came out. I said wow man, that's amazing," said Benson in an interview recorded for the Smithsonian's jazz collection of oral history. "Wow, man, that's amazing. I couldn't believe it. I went over and stuck my ear down where the speaker. The sound coming out was amazing….Fascinated, I sat right down in front of the speaker listening to the sound. So, I was hooked on the electric guitar from the very beginning."

By the time he was in the fifth grade, Benson was approached by Cephus Ford, the owner of the Little Paris Café, to play on weekends. He earned as much money—forty dollars—that his mother made every two weeks. "I was making that a night. I sang, danced and played the ukulele. People started throwing money on the stage. I said this is exciting." A police raid ended his engagement at Little Paris, and Benson ended up in juvenile court. At ten, he cut his first record as Little Georgie, "She Makes Me Mad."

He eventually dropped out of Schenley High School and started playing at Hill District joints like Mutt's Hutt. His stepfather, who was an electrician, made an electric guitar for him out of wooden top of a dresser. The only music lessons that Benson ever had was learning a few chords from Collier.

Benson left Pittsburgh, and by 1958, he was playing guitar in a go-go club in New York City. One evening, an executive from Columbia Records happened to be in the club and asked Benson to play jazz. The club owner threatened to fire any musician who played jazz, but Benson jumped onto the stage. "I played one jazz tune. That changed by life," he recounted in his autobiography. "I always wanted him to get out of Pittsburgh to play," said his mother, Erna Collier, in a 1985 *Pittsburgh Press* interview. "You never get famous if you stay local. People don't appreciate you."

Nelson Harrison

Dr. Nelson Harrison was playing the trombone professionally by the time he entered the ninth grade at Westinghouse High School. At thirteen, he was playing in a dance band at his first professional engagement at Ross's Inn. After he graduated from high school and then from the University of Pittsburgh, he was accepted to Pitt's medical school. He later quit, earning a doctorate in clinical psychology, but his musical education, however, came on streets of the Hill District. "I got my doctorate playing at the Crawford Grill," he said in a personal interview. "We learned our jazz in the community."

Nelson Harrison Quintet at Crawford Grill #2. *Courtesy of Nelson Harrison.*

Harrison learned music by listening to jazz records. "I'd sit in the dark, six to seven hours a day playing everything I heard," he said in an interview. "I was playing it on the trombone." He listened to pianist Horace Silver, trumpeters Kenny Dorham and Donald Byrd and saxophonists Hank Mobley and Lou Donaldson. "I can still do it. I still know every note on the albums."

Jazz was a dirty word at the time, and Pittsburgh's public high schools refused to include jazz in their curriculum in the 1950s. "I was walking two paths I was getting a lot of flak because I was playing jazz. I wanted to speak jazz." Harrison said jazz is a language that can convey the same feelings as the spoken word. Jazz and speech have several similarities. They both have pitch, rhythm and tempo to convey emotions, wrote Dr. David Ludden in a 2015 article in *Psychology Today* titled "Is Music A Universal Language?" Louis Armstrong, in a 1961 essay that he wrote for the *New York Times*, "Jazz Is a Language," said that "some people don't understand that the basis of jazz is a kind of language. You use it to say all kinds of things and explain all kinds of moods."

Harrison was playing a gig at the Crawford Grill in the Hill District when drummer Art Blakey was in the audience. Blakey joined Harrison on stage for a set and then told him he was impressed with his musical skills. He said, "Bonesky [a nickname for trombonists], I like what I'm hearing. Come on and go to New York with me." Harrison said he couldn't because he was in medical school at the time. "You ain't no doctor, motherfucker, you're a musician," Blakey replied.

Harrison trolled Hill District jazz clubs and knew Pittsburgh Steelers fullback John Henry Johnson, who liked jazz and had a reputation as a big spender. Harrison said he would leave home with two dollars in his pocket, find out which clubs Johnson was frequenting and tail him through the night as Johnson went from club to club. He returned home with the same amount of money in his pocket thanks to his friendship with Johnson, who played for the Steelers from 1960 to 1965.

Harrison was working on his doctorate in psychology when he received a telephone call from Eddie "Lockjaw" Davis, a saxophonist and road manager for Count Basie, telling Harrison the orchestra had an opening for

Nelson Harrison with Count Basie. Harrison turned down several chances to play with Basie before finally agreeing to join his orchestra. Harrison earned a doctorate in clinical psychology but still performs in Pittsburgh. *Courtesy of Nelson Harrison.*

a trombone player. Harrison rejected the offer because of school. He turned a second offer from Basie in 1974 and then a third two years later. Finally, Harrison joined the band in 1978 in New Orleans. "This is where I should be," Harrison recalled. It had been his dream to play with Basie one day. So, what was it like? "Heaven. In a word, heaven."

ART NANCE

Saxophonist Art Nance came from a religious family. He attended church services six nights a week and all day on Sunday where shouting and "funky" music was part of the religious ceremony, he recalled in an interview with the African American Jazz Preservation Society. Nance performed with a group in high school, playing at dances, fraternal groups, veterans' organizations and weddings "Back in those days if you got $20 for the band, we'd split it evenly. You'd get two or three dollars a night," Nance said in oral history for the Manchester Craftsmen's Guild.

Nance was twelve when he began playing the guitar but took up the sax because his dad was a saxophone player. "I wanted to play the sax. He wanted me to play the sax." Nance was returning home from school one day and found a surprise waiting for him. "I heard all this racket coming from my house. My father bought me an alto sax. That was my beginning."

After graduating from high school, Nance played at clubs around Pittsburgh with the Apollos and the Five Deuces. After he was discharged from the army, he worked for pianist Walt Harper, who owned Walt Harper's Attic, where he played full-time for a dozen years beginning in 1984.

Nance was another local artist who played with Joe Westray, a local band leader known for his eye for talent and his arrangements. Nance backed up

Dionne Warwick, Diana Ross and the Temptations, among others, during his time with Westray. Nance also worked as sidemen for Basie and guitarist Jerry Byrd and accompanied Roland Kirk, Sonny Stitt, Dizzy Gillespie and Slide Hampton. Nance eventually realized that being a full-time musician was a hard life, so he enrolled at Pitt to study accounting at night and found a job at a nursing home, rising to become the administrator while playing jazz at night.

Dodo

Michael "Dodo" Marmarosa was a superb pianist who was in and out of the spotlight for years. Born in the Larimer area of Pittsburgh, he was nicknamed because of his large head, beaked nose and small body. While he still was in high school, he began playing in East Liberty nightclubs, and at fifteen, he was touring with the Johnny "Scat" Davis Orchestra. In 1943, he and another musician, Boniface DeFranco, who later would become famous as "Buddy DeFranco," were playing with Gene Krupa in Philadelphia when they were attacked by two drunken sailors, according to accounts in the *Pittsburgh Press*, *Pittsburgh Sun-Telegraph* and *Pittsburgh Post-Gazette*. He was beaten into a coma, but after recovering, his personality changed. Marmarosa was drafted but was diagnosed as mentally ill and underwent shock treatment while in the army before he was discharged. His wife divorced him and gained custody of his two daughters.

In 1945, Marmarosa played on eighty records, including Charlie Parker's famous *Ornithology* and *Yardbird Suite* and *Night in Tunisia* with Miles Davis. He joined Artie Shaw and later was busy with recordings in Los Angeles working with Charlie Parker, Benny Carter, Lester Young and Willie Smith in 1946 and 1947. In 1947, *Esquire* magazine named him an upcoming star.

Marmarosa was eccentric and unpredictable. He once pushed a piano off the balcony of the third floor of a building just so he could hear the chord it made on smashing to pieces, according to his obituary in the *New York Times* in 2002. He was a vagabond shuffling between Pittsburgh, Chicago and the West Coast before returning to Pittsburgh and vanishing from the local jazz scene only to occasionally pop up to play at some club. His longest local engagement was at the Midway Lounge downtown, where he recorded a live album, *Dodo Marmarosa: Pittsburgh 1958*. He retired in the late 1960s, occasionally appearing at venues to play, but his last job was at the Colony. He died in 2002 at a Veterans Hospital in Pittsburgh.

FRANK CUNIMONDO

Frank Cunimondo started learning to play the piano at four, growing up in what he called an "Italian ghetto" in East Liberty. The city's east end was a wide-open neighborhood with gambling clubs, numbers joints on every block and prostitutes frequenting the clubs that were mob-run. Owners and front men were known for their violence. There were dozens of clubs in East Liberty, he said, that were packed with people who loved jazz. Even small neighborhood taverns hired jazz combos. "Pittsburgh was a wild swinging town," Cunimondo said in an interview.

While the Flamingo Lounge could accommodate hundreds, the Penn-Shady Ballroom could hold up to three thousand. When Cunimondo was just a teenager, Lenny Litman, owner of the Copa, allowed him to hang out at his club listening to jazz. He sat at the bar smoking a cigarette and nursing a beer to look older but was only fourteen. "I shouldn't have even

Frank Cunimondo performing with Mike Taylor on bass and Roger Humphries on drums. *Courtesy of Frank Cunimondo.*

been there," he recalled. "Everybody went to the Copa. Lenny was a great guy. He ran a successful operation for years."

The Motor Square Garden, which hosted a performance by Duke Ellington in 1950, was at the center of East Liberty. The majestic East Liberty Presbyterian Church was once surrounded by nightclubs and gambling dens. Among the clubs where jazz was performed included the Bachelors Club, the Lepus Literary Society and the Del Moro Canoe Club, all mob-run joints that served as fronts for gambling. Cunimondo played at several mob-run clubs where fights and beatings were not uncommon. "I played in places where you needed a gun to play in those places," he said. "Pittsburgh was a wide-open swinging town."

Don Aliquo Sr. remembered performing at the Del Moro, where "it was New Year's Eve every night. That was crazy," he recalled in an interview.

Cunimondo played every night for a year from midnight to 5:00 a.m. at the Almono and dated the girlfriends of mobsters, which may explain why Cunimondo was married and divorced three times. He said women threw themselves at musicians and he narrowly escaped beatings or worse when he began clandestinely seeing women who were dating racketeers.

Cunimondo recalled one after-hours club where he was nearly shot. A Pittsburgh police lieutenant brought his prostitute girlfriend to the club one night while Cunimondo was standing at the bar on a break. The couple got into an argument, and the girlfriend shot her lover with his service pistol nearly hitting Cunimondo.

Night life in East Liberty and other parts of Pittsburgh really didn't start he said until 2:00 a.m., when the clubs and bars closed. People would pack the Hollywood Social Club, an after-hours joint in East Liberty, where people would watch floor shows at 3:00 a.m. while eating steak and drinking.

Stanley Turrentine, Joe Westray, Jon Walton

Stanley Turrentine's father put a saxophone in his hands when he was nine years old even though a teacher at Herron Hill Jr. High School wanted him to learn the cello. "I learned how to play on the streets, at the Musicians Club," he said in an interview with the African American Jazz Preservation Society at the University of Pittsburgh.

He began playing professionally at thirteen at the Perry Bar for five dollars a weekend for Joe Westray, who was one of the most influential musicians in Pittsburgh. Westray was a guitarist, band leader, composer and arranger who served as a mentor to young musicians. After two years in the army, Turrentine joined Max Roach in 1959 and went to Europe with Roach touring and recording.

Turrentine never regretted his lack of a formal music education. "I never had to do anything else but play music. Music is something I chose to do and I did it."

Joe Westray had a formal music education and led one of the hottest bands in the city. He graduated from Carnegie Institute of Technology, now Carnegie Mellon University, and mentored young musicians. He hired Stanley Turrentine along with pianists Ahmad Jamal and Erroll Garner to play in his band. Dakota Staton was a featured vocalist for Westray in the early 1950s.

In his autobiography, *Dirt Street*, Hosea Taylor said Westray knew music and the music business. "He was a very aggressive and forceful man who was somewhat affluent—let's just say he was ghetto rich—he owned and rented all kinds of residential and commercial properties plus several trucks to handle a hauling contract with a big food chain warehouse. Joe Westray was quite the entrepreneur. He was a good role model for anyone who wished to succeed."

Westray's band was one off the three hottest Black jazz bands in Pittsburgh at one time, along with Will Hitchcock's Big Dream Band and a group led by pianist Walt Harper. Cathy Westray, Joe Westray's sister, said her brother was one of the few musicians in the Hill District who could arrange music. "Most musicians played stock arrangements, nothing original," she said in an interview on file at the Carnegie Library.

Saxophonist Jon Walton was born in Great Britain but was raised in Clairton, a steel town outside of Pittsburgh. He played with the Benny Goodman and Artie Shaw orchestras but was best known in the Pittsburgh region as one of the founding members of the Deuces Wild, a jazz combo that was popular in the late 1940s and 1950s.

Walton may have been best known for his association with the Deuces Wild, which achieved local as well as national prominence for the quality of its music. The group played six nights a week at the Midway and Carnival lounges before it morphed into two groups with the same name.

Besides Walton, the original band included saxophonist Flo Cassinelli, trombonist Tommy Turk, pianists Bobby Negri and Reid Jaynes, bassists Danny Mastri and Harry Bush and drummers Spider Rondinelli, Bill Price, Roger Ryan Dick Berosky and Carl Peticca. One version led by Turk

Roy Eldridge. *Wikipedia.*

included Bush and Berosky. A second was led by Cassinelli and included Negri, Mastri and Rondinelli. Guest artists Roy Eldridge, Coleman Hawkins and Miles Davis sometimes sat in with the group. Eldridge, who grew up in Pittsburgh's North Side, came to play a one-week engagement and ending up staying for three weeks.

Joe Negri's father, Michael, was a bricklayer who lived in the Mount Washington section of Pittsburgh overlooking the Ohio and Monongahela Rivers. He wanted both his sons to become musicians. Negri started out in show business as a singer, but "I quit show business at thirteen when my voice changed." He learned to play the guitar, while his brother, Bobby, became a jazz pianist. Negri achieved fame as world-class guitarist but also had a second career as an actor playing Handyman Negri on *Mister Rogers' Neighborhood* on public television in Pittsburgh. In 1944, Harold V. Cohen, a critic for the *Pittsburgh Post-Gazette*, mentioned Negri in one of his columns. "Young Joe Negri, a Pittsburgh lad, easily demonstrates why he is right up there with the wizards of the electric guitar."

He tried tap dancing with his brother at amateur shows and Pittsburgh theaters as the Rhythm Boys. "I was a pretty good dancer," he said in an interview. He landed a gig on KQV radio on Uncle Harry's Radio Rascals and when television came into its own, he appeared on the *Ken Griffin Show* and *Buzzy and Bill*. In 1937, Negri won third place and twenty-five dollars after playing his guitar on the *Children's Hour*, a local talent show sponsored by the Braun Baking Company.

Guitarist Joe Negri works with South Hills High School students. *University of Pittsburgh Library System.*

Negri quit high school, and by sixteen, he was performing professionally and later toured with the Shep Fields Orchestra but disliked traveling and returned to Pittsburgh. He attended Carnegie Tech in 1950 and would have graduated in 1954 if the allure of jazz hadn't led him to quit college in his junior year. He became musical director first at KDKA and later at WTAE. "My life changed when I went to Carnegie Tech in 1950," he said in an interview. "I would have graduated in 1954. I left in my junior year and started on television."

Negri wrote jingles for beer commercials while continuing to perform after his discharge from the army. He retired in 2019 at ninety-two after teaching guitar at the University of Pittsburgh for forty-nine years but continues to perform. He also taught at Duquesne and Carnegie-Mellon Universities. In 2010, he wrote *The Mass of Hope: The Jazz Idiom*. "It's quite spiritual and has a solemn depth about it. Jazz is just as valid as Bach or a piece by Chopin or anything," he said. "Without spirituality there is not creativity. Creating is a spiritual experience."

13

VOICES

Lena Horne left behind her vagabond life of trailing her actress-mother through the South before settling in Pittsburgh when she was eighteen to live with her father, Edwin Fletcher "Teddy" Horne Jr., who she described in a *Time* magazine article as "a sharp beautiful dude with a diamond stickpin." Teddy Horne was a bon vivant and gambler who was involved in the numbers racket in the Hill District with Gus Greenlee, the owner of the Crawford Grill. Lena had developed a taste for show business in New York as a fifteen-year-old chorus girl at the Cotton Club in 1933.

She lived in Pittsburgh for only four years but was married there and had two children. "She was without a doubt the queen in Pittsburgh," wrote John Brewer Jr. in his book *Pittsburgh Jazz*.

Her mother, Edna Scrotton, traveled through the South as a member of a Black theater troupe, often depositing Horne to live with relatives. Teddy Horne was protective of his daughter but supported her efforts to advance her singing career by allowing her to performing as a teenager at the Loendi Club, the Bambola and Crawford Grill and at private parties for some of the city's wealthiest families.

Her father also owned the Belmont Hotel, a place where Black musicians could stay since they were barred from white-owned hotels downtown. Her father wouldn't allow her into the hotel's cabaret, where jazz groups played, so she sat upstairs listening to the music. It was at the Belmont where she became a friend of Billy Strayhorn. Billy Strayhorn was the "only man I ever loved," Horne told the *New York Times*, and she would have married him except Strayhorn was gay.

She recounted the first meeting between her and Strayhorn in a 1993 *New York Times* article. She was sitting in a theater in 1942 feeling lonely when she was approached by "a beautiful brown boy in big horn-rimmed glasses, who looked like a lovely brown owl." He had been sent over by Ellington to see if she wanted something from the refreshment stand. "We became soul mates," she said. "Every time I have a musical crisis, I dream about him three or four days before the event." It was Strayhorn who made her a star, she said. "I wasn't born a singer. I had to learn a lot. Billy rehearsed me. He stretched me vocally."

She married at nineteen to Louis Jones, twenty-eight, who worked in a patronage job at the Allegheny County Morgue. The marriage was marked by friction and jealousy. After she went to Hollywood to appear in the film *The Duke Is Tops*, Jones refused to allow her to attend the movie's Pittsburgh premiere. The *Pittsburgh Courier* savaged Horne by revealing she went to see a "white" movie the night of the premiere and hinted that the reason she refused to appear was because she wanted paid for her attendance. While praising her singing in the movie, the paper noted "as an actress she is no Myrna Loy." Jones filed for divorce, claiming desertion, but the two reconciled only to end their marriage in 1944.

Horne refused Hollywood job offers to play maids or prostitutes in films and was viewed by producers as difficult to work with. She became a civil rights advocate and once walked out of a USO show for German POWs in Arkansas after Black soldiers were barred from attending.

Horne's skin tone caused her career problems. When she was a child, her light-colored complexion prompted Black children to accuse her of having a "white daddy," according to a *New York Times* article after she died in 2010. In movies, directors tried to darken her skin so moviegoers wouldn't mistake her for white.

Horne went to Hollywood to make movies for MGM and was paid $1,000 a week. She also earned $1,500 every time she sang on radio and $6,500 for a week-long nightclub engagement. Then her career took a turn. She was blacklisted from movies and television for several years during the McCarthy era after her name appeared in "Red Channels: The Report of Communist Influence in Radio and Television," a publication listing known communists or sympathizers. Her friendship with singer and actor Paul Robeson, a suspected communist, and her willingness to defend blacklisted writers in Hollywood also damaged her career prospects. Membership in the Communist Party didn't matter to anti-communist zealots who believed mere suspicion was enough to taint a person as a fellow traveler.

Controversy continued to follow Horne after it was revealed that she had secretly married a white man, Lennie Hayton, the musical director for MGM, in 1947 but didn't announce the union publicly until 1950.

Louise Mann could fill a room with the sound of her singing voice without using a microphone. The *Pittsburgh Courier* dubbed her the "princess of mirth" when she died in 1939. Her funeral in the city was huge, according to the *Courier.* The procession was led by a seventy-five-car cortege. Among the musicians sending their condolences were Sullivan, Duke Ellington, Fats Waller and Roy Eldridge.

Mann got her start playing the piano at the Benjamin Harrison Literary Society, a mob-run after-hours club on Liberty Avenue, where the gambling was done in a back room hidden behind a thick drape. Mann jammed with Earl Hines, Casey Harris, Fletcher Henderson and James "Honey Boy" Minor at Derby Dan's, the Collins Inn, the Humming Bird, the Fullerton Inn and the Paradise Inn.

A young pianist who spelled Mann during breaks at the club was Marietta Williams, who changed her name to Maxine Sullivan and became a major singing star. Sullivan worked as a waitress and singer at the Benjamin Harrison Literary Society after graduating from Homestead High School. She told jazz critic Leonard Feather of the *Los Angeles Times* in 1987 that the club was "one of those 'knock three times, who's there?' places…I went to work at 11 p.m. and worked until unconscious, singing from table to table, you know, 99 choruses of 'Dinah' or whatever. It was a good experience and it paid $14 a week plus tips."

At the age of six, Sullivan was entered into a singing contest by her mother at the Carnegie Library in Homestead singing "I'm Forever Blowing Bubbles.' Sullivan began singing in her uncle's band, the Red Hot Peppers, when she was discovered by Gladys Mosier, a pianist in Ina Ray Hutton's all-female band, who urged Sullivan to move to New York City. Sullivan took her advice, and Mosier introduced her to composer Claude Thornhill in the 1930s.

That meeting led to a record deal, where Sullivan recorded the tune that made her most famous" the Scottish folk song "Loch Lomond." Sullivan had "a voice as soothing as a gust of wind on a balmy summer day," noted the *Pittsburgh Courier* in 1946.

Thornhill was looking for a specific song that would ignite Sullivan's career, and "Loch Lomond" did just that and propelled Sullivan to prominence during the swing era. In 1937, the *Pittsburgh Courier* wrote that she "put in the 'ing' in swing." The hit song led to a job at CBS Radio and then to

Maxine Sullivan started her singing career in an after-hours club in Pittsburgh. She achieved fame when she recorded the Scottish ballad "Loch Lomond." *Library of Congress.*

Hollywood, where she made two movies. She later appeared on Broadway starring in *Swinging the Dream*, a jazz version of Shakespeare's *A Midsummer Night's Dream*, with Louis Armstrong and Benny Goodman. She went off the musical grid in 1957 to devote herself to her children, their school and the PTA but came out of retirement returning to singing in 1967.

Other female jazz artists who achieved local fame but opted to remain in Pittsburgh included Lum Sams, a singer with the Deuces Wild who worked with guitarist Joe Negri, trombonists Harold Betters and Tommy Turk, trumpet player Danny Conn and pianist Walt Harper in the late 1950s and 1960s. Betters, who was known locally as "Mr. Trombone," was a fixture at the Encore in Pittsburgh's Shadyside neighborhood in the 1960s. He said he never regretted remaining close to home because he was able to spend more time with his family. Nevertheless, he jammed at Pittsburgh clubs with jazz greats like Max Roach, Dizzy Gillespie, Stanley Turrentine, Roy Eldridge and Sonny Rollins. Betters died on October 11, 2020, at ninety-two.

Nightclubs billed Sams as "Pittsburgh's famous singer," according to ads in the *Pittsburgh Press*. Jessie Wills was an attractive redhead who "could improvise like nobody," said Frank Cunimondo, who accompanied Wills.

The late Sandy Staley grew up singing as a baby. Her acts were characterized by fashionable gowns and long, dangling earrings. Cunimondo accompanied Staley on singing engagements and once was "the top jazz singer in Pittsburgh." He said Staley was a heavy smoker and had to inhale oxygen from a portable tank during breaks so she would be able to continue singing. "She was the queen of Pittsburgh. She was an unbelievable singer," Cunimondo said. "She was the boss. She could improvise like nobody."

He said singers Etta Cox, Sandy Dowe (a voice professor at Duquesne University) and the late Maureen Budway would have been major stars if they hadn't decided to remain in Pittsburgh. Marva Josie, who was from Clairton, started her career singing gospel and later joined the Earl Hines Orchestra.

Dakota Staton was a tall, curvy woman who liked to drink scotch and milk with ice. She was another of the musical wonders from Westinghouse High School and sounded like Dinah Washington. "I don't like to say I have a particular style. I just like to sing," she told the *Pittsburgh Press* in a 1958 interview. "She has a punchy, declamatory delivery which is her tie to Miss Washington, but she also has a rich vibrant voice that lifts toward an emphatic shout, and assurance and color in her delivery that are distinctively her own," wrote a music critic for the *New York Times* in 1978. "Miss Staton is a commanding presence who conjures up the classic blues singer of the 20s."

After leaving Westinghouse, Staton formed a trio with her sisters until they married. Then she joined a band led by Joe Westray. "I used to sing in local spots, with Joe Westray's band, went to Detroit, then to New York and that's where a disc jockey heard me sing and I made an album." Actually, it was a producer for Capitol Records who heard her sing at the Baby Grand nightclub and signed her to a contract on the spot. By the time she was twenty-three, Staton was a star, and *Downbeat* magazine named her among the most promising new artists in 1955.

Her first album, *The Late, Late Show*, reached number four on the music charts in 1957. The *New York Times* followed her career because she was a fixture in the city's nightclubs and cabarets. In 1998, a critic called Staton "one of America's great vocal stylists."

LIFE AT THE KEYBOARD

by Francine Costello

"It's a cozy little corner where I am." Frank Cunimondo is a world class jazz piano player and his "cozy corner" is here in Western Pennsylvania in our part of the Allegheny River valley. After years of traveling with bands "on the road," working the big jazz clubs of New York City and the resorts of South Florida, making that all-important appearance on the Johnny Carson show, Cunimondo is an artist fulfilled. And that fulfillment came after he stopped the travelling, brought it all home and made it happen here.

He plays the music he loves in his own club in Verona. He teaches jazz at Duquesne University, using the textbook he wrote. He publishes his own albums and tapes. He writes and arranges, makes plans and directs the world he's created from his comfortable home in Natrona Heights. It's all done on Cunimondo's turf, in Cunimondo's style with a low flame that belies the intensity and magnitude of the talent this man possesses and shares so readily.

The year is 1952. A steely, March wind is sweeping the Atlantic City Boardwalk. Three teenagers, their coats billowing behind them, walk, heads down and carry their musical instruments from saloon to saloon, looking for summer work. They want to play their music for the big crowds in the big city on the shore. But it's been a day of rejection. No one is interested in three college kids from Pittsburgh who play serious jazz. Tired, cold and hungry, the piano player, the drummer and the base fiddle player try one last place, The Clock Bar, at the far end of the Boardwalk. "When the guy said fine, I'm hiring you, we just freaked-out!" Frank Cunimondo will tell you with an excitement in his voice that makes it hard to believe this inconspicious beginning so many years ago, still means so much to him. But it does. As does everything having to do with his music.

By the age of twelve Cunimondo was actively involved in jazz. He played the classics on the piano with dedication but he worked with fascination, at his jazz. When he entered the seventh grade at Westinghouse High School the young piano player found a home. There, at

HE PLAYS THE MUSIC HE LOVES IN HIS OWN CLUB IN VERONA.

Westinghouse was one of the first and perhaps one of the country's greatest high school swing bands, the Cadets, pronounced the Kay'-dets.

"In that band were future stars," remembers Cunimondo, "Ahmad Jamal who was then Freddy Jones and Dakota Staton were in that band. The Aris Brothers who later played with Count Basie, played for the Cadets. Some really unbelievable musicians were in that band at that time. So this high school band was better than some professional bands you'd find touring around the country."

Predictably, young Frank Cunimondo was destined for the Cadets. To this day he still remembers the first moment he heard this remarkable band play. The number was "Blue Flame" and at the opening notes, the twelve year old boy piano player in the audience said, "That's it, that's what I want to do, that's my life." Jazz.

Music dominated Cunimondo's school years, both in school and out of school. He joined every musical group and band at Westinghouse and after hours he earned money playing the piano with a small group he formed. So by the age of thirteen, Frank Cunimondo was playing professionally for weddings and other affairs. When he was fifteen, Cunimondo landed a six night a week job playing piano with his own trio every night from nine until two in the morning at Genovese Cocktail Lounge in East Liberty.

By the time Frank Cunimondo entered Carnegie Tech for college, he had been a professional musician for many years. He had even gone "on the road" with a band for the summer, touring Canada. So when he entered college in the fall, Cunimondo says he was bored by college life. That's when he conceived the idea of bringing his trio out of town to play for the summer. They chose Philadelphia by looking on a map for the closest big city to Pittsburgh. Armed with the names of key people in clubs and lounges in Philadelphia, the three took their instruments and headed east. But when they got to Philly, Joe in this club and Nick in that bar all told them the same thing; the place to go for summer jobs is Atlantic City. And so it was.

Back at Carnegie Tech that fall, still playing nights at the Genovese Lounge, Cunimondo was even more discouraged with school. In those years, only classical music was studied at the college level and Cunimondo already knew that it was jazz that was his destiny and nothing else. In April though, his break came. A musician hearing him play one night suggested he audition for the famous Billy May Orchestra who was appearing at the Ches-a-rena the next night. The man told Cunimondo who he should contact and that Frank could use his name. "I just went and talked to the guy," Cunimondo remembers, "and on the strength of my friend's recommendation, they said, "whenever there's an opening we'll call you." So without as much as playing one note, two weeks later Cunimondo got a telegram asking him to join the band. "Man," he says, "I didn't think twice."

But life on the road for a nineteen year old wasn't easy. The band played all the country's big ballrooms and that meant a different city every night. For Cunimondo, it was a lonely life. The musicians were all older than he and they shared nothing but their music. "It was just one city after another and maybe every third night you'd stay in a hotel." Then it was back on the bus and more traveling. So here was this boy, this kid from Pittsburgh, sitting up nights, alone and awake on a bus carrying musicians from city to city to play their music in the big ballrooms that would soon go dark as their grand moment in history was about to end.

WHY DO YOU HAVE TO LEAVE HOME AND YOUR SURROUNDINGS TO DO SOMETHING. WHY CAN'T IT BE DONE IN PITTSBURGH

When Cunimondo left the Billy May band he returned to Pittsburgh and played the local clubs. But as it happens with most artists, the allure of New York City and its rich offerings was irresistable. And New York was a good move for Cunimondo. His talent was quickly recognized, he was almost immediately

Frank Cunimondo often accompanied singer Sandy Staley when she was performing. *Courtesy of Frank Cunimondo.*

Tiny Irvin was with Dizzy Gillespie in 1949 and 1950 performing with Sammy Davis Jr., Carmen McRae and Sarah Vaughan. Irvin returned to Pittsburgh, where she married and had a son. She decided to go back into show business and traveled to New York to find an agent but received a less-than-enthusiastic response. When she learned that Gillespie was performing at the Village Gate, she went to the club and told the doorman, "Tell Diz that Tiny's here." Gillespie was overjoyed to see her and asked her to perform that night. She stole the show.

"She reached the audience so quickly that, within a few bars, her listeners had picked up her beat and were clapping along with her," wrote John S. Wilson in a review in the *New York Times* in 1968. In Pittsburgh, Irvin worked the major nightspots, including the Zebra Room, Horizon Door, Midway Lounge, the Balcony, the Tender Trap, Hollywood Show Bar and Rusty Scupper. She retired in the late 1980s.

Delsey McKay sang with the Duke Ellington Orchestra in the late 1960s and then moved to New York before touring Europe and then returning to Pittsburgh. She graduated from Duquesne University and Juilliard and was known in jazz circles as the "Sepia Doll." Michele Bensen was born in Chicago but raised in Pittsburgh, where she has remained. She first appeared on the city's music scene in 1973, when Pittsburgh entertainment writer George Anderson of the *Pittsburgh Post-Gazette* caught her act at the Encore with trombonist Harold Betters. "She is the most exciting singer I've heard in a long while," wrote Anderson.

Vivian Reed sang jazz and appeared on Broadway after leaving Pittsburgh noted the *New York Times* in 1976 when she appeared in the Broadway musical *Bubbling Brown Sugar*. "She belongs to a mode of Broadway gospel-schooled belters who transfer pop songs into spiritual testament," wrote critic Stephen Holden in the *Times*. In 2015, Holden called Reed "an heir to Lena Horne in the cold firepower of her majestic rage."

Spanky Wilson was born Louella Wilson in Philadelphia but grew up in Pittsburgh. She performed with Stanley Turrentine and Jimmy McGriff and was a backup singer for Lou Rawls. She also shared the stage with Marvin Gaye and Sammy Davis Jr. She was greeted with boos when she appeared at a music festival in Brazil in 1970 but soon had the crowd cheering when she started singing reported *Jet* magazine.

Joyce Breech's connection to Pittsburgh is at best tenuous, but she has had an effect on the cabaret scene in New York City. She was born in California, raised in Kansas City and lived in the city while she attended West Virginia University. She grew up listening to Judy Garland, Sarah Vaughan, Peggy

Lee and Frank Sinatra, and her act features tunes from the Great American Songbook of composers George Gershwin, Cole Porter, Irving Berlin, Jerome Kern, Harold Arlen, Johnny Mercer and Richard Rodgers.

"She could sing her butt off," Cunimondo said. In 2014, the *New York Times* said Breech "is a quintessential keeper of the flame of an intimate nightclub tradition that flickers mostly under the mass-media radar." In 2011, the Huffington Post called her "a world-class pop singer you never heard of."

Phyllis Hyman was born in Philadelphia and raised in Pittsburgh. After she graduated from Carrick High School in the city's South Hills, she received a scholarship to Robert Morris University but stayed only a year before touring as a singer with a group, New Edition. She was working days as a legal secretary when a friend persuaded her to audition.

She recorded her first album at twenty-eight, *Prime of My Life*, and then had a hit single "You Know How to Love Me," following by more albums from the late 1970s until the early 1990s. Hyman also was an actress, appearing on Broadway and in three movies: *School Daze* by Spike Lee and *The Killer Reflex* and *Too Scared To Scream*.

The *New York Times* called Hyman a "remarkable singer. One moment she is tenderly burning a deep, golden note, the next she is belting out a chorus with a brassy blare." In an interview with her hometown *Pittsburgh Press* in 1983, she admitted getting into jazz by chance: "The jazz thing was something I didn't work at. It just came. I didn't know whether it sounded right but I guess I had the right vocal inflections. A couple of years ago an old-time jazz pianist heard me sing and said, 'You know what you are? You're a jazz singer.'"

Hyman was a natural beauty, appearing on the covers of *Jet* magazine in 1981 and again ten years later, but beneath the surface she was struggling with mental illness and addictions to cocaine and alcohol. She was in and out of rehab several times, and the addictions caused her weight to balloon to three hundred pounds. Several hours before she was scheduled to perform at the Apollo Theater in Harlem, Hyman took an overdose of pentobarbital and secobarbital. She was forty-five. In a note she left behind, she wrote: "I'm tired. I'm tired. Those of you that I love, you know who you are. May God bless you."

14

PROMOTERS

They helped promote jazz in Pittsburgh even though their names are little more than a footnote in the city's musical history. Gus Greenlee was king of the numbers racket in the city's Hill District, raking in millions of dollars off the pennies of the poor and desperate. Sellers McKee Hall was a promoter and nightclub owner. Harry Collins was a successful businessman who was convicted of drug dealing and served time in a federal prison. Harry Hendel was a shrewd businessman and nightclub owner who had an eye for talent.

Ann Simmons Dunlap couldn't play a note of music, but she knew people who could. Dunlap, known as "Birdie," owned the Hurricane Lounge, which was known for its music, pretty waitresses and her Brazilian fried shrimp. Lenny Litman owned several successful nightclubs in the downtown area and booked big-name acts such as Art Tatum, Erroll Garner, Ethel Waters, George Shearing, Mary Lou Williams, Johnny Mathis, Ella Fitzgerald, Count Basie, Duke Ellington, Woody Herman, Miles Davis and Artie Shaw.

Tony Mowod, known as the "godfather of jazz" in Pittsburgh, promoted the music through decades of radio, playing jazz nightly on WDUQ-FM until Duquesne University sold the station in 2011. Mowod founded the Pittsburgh Jazz Society and helped promote the Mellon Jazz Festival.

Greenlee was a bootlegger, bookie, gambler, boxing promoter, baseball club owner and businessman, but he made his name as a jazz impresario at his Crawford Grill, which became a must-stop for touring musicians such as Art Blakey, Charles Mingus, Max Roach, Miles Davis and John

Coltrane. The Grill also served as a launching pad for young Pittsburgh-based artists. Greenlee owned a number of businesses during his lifetime. His holdings included two hotels, a pool hall and the Sunset Café. He later purchased the Paramount Inn, remodeled it and reopened the club on Christmas Eve 1933 as the Crawford Grill, the first of three establishments to bear the name.

Legend has it that before he opened the Crawford Grill, Greenlee and William "Woogie" Harris introduced the numbers racket to Pittsburgh, and it made them wealthy men. In 1926, the two were arrested by police, who were unsure what to charge them with. They were accused of operating a lottery, fined $100 and released. The new racket quickly spread across the city, raking in thousands of dollars a day and enabling Greenlee to buy restaurants and bars before investing in the Pittsburgh Crawfords and building his own baseball stadium in 1928.

The *Pittsburgh Press* estimated the racket generated between $20,000 and $25,000 a day, earning Greenlee and Harris $2 million in 1928. Numbers writers working for Greenlee and Harris trolled the streets collecting pennies, nickels and dimes from desperate people hoping to cash in on a winning number; they then waited for the "stock" edition of one of the city's newspapers to hit the streets in the late afternoon to see if their selection hit. People quickly turned to the business pages looking for the three-combination of numbers from the New York Stock Exchange that would indicate the winning number. People consulted spiritualists who were paid quarter for a "dream number" that they foresaw in their sleep.

The history of how the game came into being in the city is unclear, but the numbers racket was a scourge in Pittsburgh for decades, igniting gang wars for control of the multi-million-dollar criminal enterprise. The money generated by the numbers spread corruption among politicians and law enforcement officials. The Grill likely was a front for Greenlee's gambling operation, wrote Colter Harper in his doctoral dissertation.

He served in the U.S. Army during World War I as a machine gunner, and Greenlee's wealth from the numbers made him an important man in the Hill. He became a de facto bank, lending money to Black residents of the Hill who couldn't get a mortgage from white-run banks to buy homes. He fed people during the Great Depression and quietly lobbied for an end to segregation in baseball, paving the way for Jackie Robinson. He wore custom-made white suits, black shirts and white shoes that made him look like a gangster. Friends called him "Big Red" because of his size, reddish-colored hair and freckles.

On weekends, Pittsburgh's elite white clientele, such as Art Rooney, who owned the Pittsburgh Steelers, or the department store owner Edgar Kaufmann went to the Crawford Grill on weekends, according to a 2015 article, "Taking Its Bow," in the *Carnegie*, a magazine published by the Carnegie Museum of Modern Art. Rooney and Greenlee were close friends because of their ties through sports, according to the Society for American Baseball Research. The Crawford Grill No. 2 became a hangout for politicians, police officials and athletes such as Satchell Paige and Josh Gibson of the Pittsburgh Crawfords baseball team and later Roberto Clemente and Willie Stargell of the Pittsburgh Pirates.

Black and white patrons mixed easily in the Crawford Grill because it was the music that drew them to the club. Dr. Ralph Proctor, a history professor at the Community College of Allegheny County in Pittsburgh, said most of the customers were white. "The grill provided a place of elegance in an area outsiders tended to think as down-trodden. One could dress in elegant outfits, hearing elegant music, eat elegant food while escaping the surroundings filled with racial hatred," Proctor said in "Taking Its Bow."

"Its reputation extended far beyond its physical boundaries and many white folks came to hear the music, let their hair down, and eat the famous chicken wings. For many whites it was the first time they came to realize that we were a vibrant people full of hope and dreams despite oppressing racism."

Greenlee's later years were filled with health and legal problems. He was arrested for gambling and voter fraud. He had trouble with the IRS over back taxes. Greenlee became ill in 1950, and the original Crawford Grill burned down, never to be rebuilt. Greenlee died in 1952 without knowing the grill had been destroyed.

Sellers McKee Hall was an athlete who starred in track, football, baseball and basketball before he became the first Black music promoter in Pittsburgh in the 1920s, booking Duke Ellington, Billy Eckstine, Fletcher Henderson, Cab Calloway, Noble Sissle, Chick Webb, Jimmy Lunceford and Andy Kirk to play at the Labor Temple, the Temple Casino and the New Dreamland in the Hill District. His father was George Hall, who founded the Loendi Club, a social and literary organization for the Hill District's Black elite who were known as "old Pittsburghers."

Hall took over the Pythian Temple, one of the most popular spots for jazz, from the Knights of Pythias. The venue became a must-stop for touring bands. Hall staged all-night shows featuring two bands. One played until 2:00 a.m. and the other until sunrise.

Hall loved baseball and played for the legendary Homestead Grays in the National Negro League and later owned and played for the Pittsburgh American Giants and later the Cuban-X Giants. He turned to journalism in 1912, writing for the *Pittsburgh Courier*. In 1924, he turned to music promotion, creating a booking agency, the Temple Amusement Company. He once told the *Pittsburgh Courier* that he had made and lost $500,000 promoting jazz dances in his career. Hall had a dozen children but divorced his wife in 1922 and moved to Chicago in 1939. He was arrested and brought back to Pittsburgh for failing to pay child support, according to the *Pittsburgh Courier*.

Harry Collins made a fortune during the Great Depression running a speakeasy in the Hill District. The Collins Inn was notorious for its nightlife and sale of illegal liquor from 1919 to the end of Prohibition in 1933. The inn was one of the more luxurious black and tan clubs on the Hill, but Collins had strict rules. Only couples were allowed in—no single men or women. When Mayor William Magee and Public Safety Director George McCandless tried to enter the club, they were barred. No exceptions, Collins said. The real reason for the police crackdown was because "white and black couples mixed freely," according to a 1922 edition of the *Pittsburgh Post*. Collins died in New York. He had no family to grieve him, but Lois Deppe came to the funeral and sang for the man who had given him his break in show business.

Henry Hendel, a blunt businessman, acquired the Pythian Temple from fellow promoter Sellers McKee Hall in 1937. Hendel at one time owned the Roosevelt Theater, the Savoy Ballroom and the Granada Theater, all in the Hill District. He renamed the temple the New Granada Theater. He closed the Savoy Ballroom in 1945 and opened the New Savoy Ballroom. By the mid-1960s, jazz had lost its luster, and the ballroom began booking rhythm and blues acts.

The *Courier* noted that Hendel financed one of the first Hollywood movies to cast singer Lena Horne, who began her singing career in the Hill District, in a leading role. He also took a financial risk in building the Roosevelt Theater after investors thought building a venue to cater to Black audiences was like "chasing will of the wisp rainbow," the *Courier* reported.

It cost Hendel $400,000 to build the theater, and he refused to allow segregated seating. Hendel, who was Jewish, was a power in the Hill District because of his business acumen and was progressive in his thinking. Someone circulated flyers throughout the Hill in 1933 under Hendel's name informing the public that the new seating policy required Black patrons to sit in the balcony while the main floor was reserved for white attendees.

The New Granada Theater at Centre Ave and DeVilliers Street was built in 1927. The theater was built by promoter Harry Hendel as the place for African Americans to gather to hear jazz greats such as Ella Fitzgerald, Count Basie, Cab Calloway and Duke Ellington, among many other performers, since Black people were not allowed in downtown Pittsburgh theaters and clubs. *University of Pittsburgh Digital Library System.*

Hendel responded with a story in the *Pittsburgh Courier* debunking the so-called policy: "There is no Jim-Crow in this house, there never had been and there never will be as long as I am in control."

Black people in the Hill District appreciated his policy and filled his theaters for shows featuring Noble Sissle and the Billy Eckstine orchestras. "Harry Hendel, to the negroes of Pittsburgh, is a bigger man than his theaters because the people realize that to the man—and not house—do they owe their allegiance," the *Courier* wrote.

When they were performing in Pittsburgh, Duke Ellington, Count Basie and Sarah Vaughan would stop in the Hurricane Lounge after their engagements had ended. Pittsburgh Steelers quarterback Bobby Layne and his entourage of teammates and drinking buddies, Gene "Big Daddy" Lipscomb, Ernie Stautner and John Henry Johnson, would hit the club on a Saturday night. Layne would run up a bar tab of $600 and then drop two crisp $100 bills into the saxophone of Jay McNeely on the way out the door, according to a 1984 *Pittsburgh Press* story.

Birdie Dunlap was reportedly a descendant of Sally Hemings, the mistress of Thomas Jefferson, through the Woodson family, according to various

Fulton Theater, Sixth Street and Duquesne Way in November 1937. *University of Pittsburgh Library System.*

Loew's United Artist Theater, Federal Street and Penn Avenue. *Pittsburgh City Photographer Collection, University of Pittsburgh Digital Library System.*

historical accounts. However, DNA testing revealed none of the Woodsons had any genetic links to either Hemings or Jefferson, according to Anne Gordon-Reed's 1998 book, *The Hemingses of Monticello: An American Family.*

Dunlap hand-rolled cigars at thirteen; was married at fifteen to her first husband, who later died; worked as a maid; and turned to music promotion in 1935, booking acts in Pittsburgh such as Louis Armstrong and Fats Waller at the Motor Square Garden in East Liberty. She once booked Ella Fitzgerald at the Club Mirador. She gave up the music business and married her second husband, William "Shine" Dunlap, who opened the Hurricane Lounge.

The audience at the Hurricane was diverse. In 1984, the Pittsburgh Press described the patrons who came to the lounge as "guys who never had a nickel and never would; guys who were rolling in the dough and all the schemers and dreamers in between women who were knockouts; and women who used to be and women who were to be and women who were hard and fast and out for a good time."

Dunlap ran a tight ship. She wouldn't allow prostitutes or known drug peddlers into her club and "none of them sissy boys either." She packed strangers—Black and white—together at tables and booths in her small club.

The Hurricane was noted for its lack of racial tension. "I just can't explain it to you because segregation and prejudice was rampant," she said in a 1984 *Pittsburgh Press* interview. "But everybody would be sitting together in the same booth. And I had a good time with 'em."

Dunlap helped legitimize the organ as a jazz instrument by launching the careers of Jimmy Smith and Jimmy McGriff as well as Johnny "Hammond" Smith, Gene Ludwig of Pittsburgh and Jack McDuff, who first popularized the Hammond B-3 Organ and made the instrument acceptable in jazz circles.

Lenny Litman had been a press agent, sportswriter and then publicist for cowboy movie star Hoot Gibson before getting into the nightclub business. He opened Mercur's Music Bar in 1944 in the city's Market Square after serving in the U.S. Navy. One of his favorite acts was pianist Art Tatum, who liked to perform in Pittsburgh because he had friends in the Hill District, said Litman in an oral history recorded for the National Council of Jewish Women at the University of Pittsburgh. He considered Tatum the great jazz pianist of all time. "He was in a class of his own. Nobody could come close to him....He was the greatest."

In 1948, Litman sold Mercur's and purchased the Villa Madrid, which later became the Copa, a popular Liberty Avenue club. The Copa closed on New Year's Eve 1959 because of the rising cost of salaries of artists.

The fee for an artist depended on popularity. He said Billy Eckstine in 1948 demanded $1,200 for a week, but Litman refused to pay because he didn't think Eckstine was worth the price.

He paid Ella Fitzgerald $1,200 for a week's stay but shelled out $3,000 when Nat King Cole played the Copa. "He was the highest I paid anybody at the Copa." Harry Belafonte was a flop when he performed an imitation of Billy Eckstine. "Son," Litman told him. "Don't you think you ought to get into another line of work?"

After he closed the Copa, Litman opened the Midway Lounge, which attracted stars like Roy Eldridge, Anita O'Day, Art Blakey, Marian McPartland, Dodo Marmaroso, Dave Brubeck, Sonny Rollins, Tiny Irvin, Walt Harper and Chet Baker. From there, it was all downhill.

By the early 1970s, the Midway had become a strip joint with waitresses with teased hair and tinted leotards. The acts featured an aging Sally Rand, known for her peek-a-boo ostrich feather fan dance; the Gay Deceivers, female impersonators; Rico the Mighty Midget; and strippers Diva Devine and Mona Lisa. The Midway later became a go-go bar, a gay bar and, in the 1980s, the Venture Inn.

Tony Mowod was born Najeeba Samreny and raised in the Hill District, and he had jazz in his DNA. He tried his hand at being a jazz musician, playing the piano and vibraphone, but his contribution to the city's jazz culture was through radio, not as an artist. Mowod was the longtime host of a jazz program on WDUQ-FM at Duquesne University until the station was sold in 2011 to Essential Public Media, which operates WESA-FM, an all-news station. He fell in love with the music by accident.

"When the kids all were listening to rock and roll, I happened to hear some things by Stan Getz, Johnny Smith, then Art Tatum and Charlie Parker. There was something exciting about music," he said in a 1988 interview in the *Pittsburgh Post-Gazette.*

Mowod, who founded the Pittsburgh Jazz Society, hosted a show, *The Nite Side*, Monday through Friday. His soft voice and laid-back style kept listeners involved in jazz. His show was syndicated to forty radio markets.

"My thinking of being a disc jockey is not just to play continuous music. It's important to talk about the music so that if you do play something a little bit heavy, the person who isn't into it can understand," he told the *Pittsburgh Press* in 1988. "I am committed to jazz in Pittsburgh because we have had more musicians coming out of this town than just about anywhere else. We're probably second only to Detroit."

15

MUSIC TO DIE FOR

Conrad Yeatis Clark was born in poverty in a grimy coal patch in southwestern Pennsylvania, but as Sonny Clark, he became one of the most highly influential and least-known jazz pianists during his short life. He died at thirty-one due to an overdose of heroin, a drug that has gone hand in hand with jazz since the bebop era.

Clark was born in 1931, one of eight children to a coal miner in Herminie No. 2, a village that was built by the Ocean Coal Company in Westmoreland County east of Pittsburgh. Towns in the bituminous coal region of southwestern Pennsylvania all looked alike, and Clark lived in one of the rows of cheaply built wooden frame houses near gob piles of sandstone and shale, the spoils of mining. Southeast of Pittsburgh, Herminie was one of dozens of coal patches that dotted the Westmoreland Coal field with names like Dorothy, Marguerite, Standard Shaft and Heckla. Herminie had a school, a tavern, a company store, a hotel and a few churches. Coal was king when Clark was born, and most of these hardscrabble villages were populated by Slavs and Italians with a few Black families.

After his father, Emory Clark, died two weeks after Clark was born, Clark's mother, Ruth Shepherd Clark, moved the family to the nearby Rosewood Inn, a twenty-two-room hotel owned by John Rosewood, where Clark had the opportunity to learn to play the piano and listen to jazz bands play there at weekend dances.

The family moved to Pittsburgh, where he performed in the "Night of Stars" at the Syria Mosque in 1946 on a bill that included Earl Hines, Mary

Lou Williams, Erroll Garner, Billy Eckstine, Roy Eldridge, Ray Brown, Lois Deppe and Maxine Sullivan. Clark must have left an impression with the audience because the *Pittsburgh Courier* referred to his performance as "twelve years of sheer genius," thinking Clark was twelve when he really was fifteen. Sam Stephenson wrote about the event in "Sonny Clark: Melody and Melancholy" in the Jazz Loft Project.

Clark carved out a reputation as an in-demand jazz pianist, recording with Charles Mingus, Stanley Turrentine and Paul Chambers. Clark was a difficult man to understand, although fans loved his artistry. "Even to his cult admirers, he is a bit of a cipher, more easily loved than understood," wrote Nate Chinen, a former jazz critic for the *New York Times* in an article for the website of station WBGO in Newark, New Jersey, in 2017.

Stephenson, who produces the Jazz Loft Project, quoted a fellow musician of Clark's describing Clark's addiction to heroin and the effect it had on his music:

> *One of the saddest sights these days is the terrible condition of one of the nation's foremost, and certainly original pianists. Having been around for many years he came into his own in 1959 and no one deserved it more than he. I feel that something should be done about drug addiction before we lose many more artists. I saw him several times in the past three months and was shocked to see one of our jazz greats in such pitiful shape. Unfortunately, the album dates that he keeps getting only help his addiction get worse instead of better. Whether or not he licks this problem at this stage of the game remains to be seen. In some cases, people refuse help and the loss of a close friend was no help either.*

Clark reportedly finished his set at Junior's, a bar in the Alvin Hotel, and then collapsed on January 13, 1963. The hotel was located in Manhattan at Fifty-Second and Broadway, once the home of a series of jazz clubs, the Band Box, Birdland, Bop City and Café Zanzibar. Stephenson writes that he suspected that hotel employees moved Clark's body to an apartment rather than leaving him at the bar to avoid bad publicity.

Drugs and alcohol have led to the deaths of a number of famous jazz artists at young ages; they suffered from heart and liver diseases, lung cancer, tuberculosis and pneumonia brought on by addiction.

Heroin contributed to the deaths of Fats Navarro, twenty-six; Billie Holiday, forty-four; Lee Morgan, thirty-three; Charlie Parker, thirty-four; John Coltrane, forty; and Fats Waller, twenty-nine. Pittsburgh musicians were not immune. The drug killed bassist Paul Chambers at thirty-three. Drummers Art Blakey and Tommy Turrentine (brother of Stanley Turrentine) and saxophonist Jon Walton, who played in the Pittsburgh-based Deuces Wild, were addicts. Walton was arrested for heroin possession after finishing a set at a nightclub.

Jazz artists have used references to drugs and alcohol in their music for decades. Cab Calloway's "Reefer Man" and "Minnie the Moocher" refer to the use of marijuana and cocaine. Singer Victoria Spivey sang about heroin in "Dope Head Blues." In 1936, Snuff Smith wrote "Here Comes the Man with the Jive," a reference to a drug dealer. Harry "The Hipster" Gibson recorded "Who Put the Benzedrine in Mrs. Murphy's Ovaltine?" in 1947.

Novelist Nelson Algren wrote the novel *The Man with the Golden Arm*, which was made into a movie starring Frank Sinatra as a card shark and morphine addict who gets clean and tries to get a job as a drummer only to fall back to his drug habit.

Heroin once was a patent medicine used in cough syrup. It was easy to obtain without a prescription until the 1950s. It was advertised as a cure for morphine addiction, but users failed to realize that heroin was a highly concentrated form of morphine. Heroin provides the user with a feeling of euphoria, warmth and relaxation, but it also lowers a person's blood pressure, causes shallow breathing and a slower heart rate. An overdose will cut off oxygen to the brain and cause death.

Clark was in demand as a musician in the 1950s and 1960s, recording *Cool Struttin'*, *Dial "S" for Sonny* and *Sonny's Crib*. He appeared in a 1956 television episode of the ABC series *Stars of Jazz*, but the tape was lost, according to Aaron Gilbreath's "The Lost Footage of Pianist Sonny Clark" in the *Michigan Quarterly Review* in 2016.

Another more compelling audiotape surfaced that depicted the depth of Clark's heroin addiction. Photographer W. Eugene Smith, the father of the photographic essay, taped a variety of conversations ranging from street noise to telephone calls to random conversations when he was living in a loft on Sixth Avenue in New York City. Smith once lived in Pittsburgh, spending two years taking thirteen thousand pictures of Pittsburgh for a photographic essay of the city.

He placed microphones in the hallway and stairway of his loft to capture the ordinary conversations of people entering and leaving the building. One dialogue Smith captured was in September 1961 when Clark lay moaning on the floor following an overdose of heroin. A fellow musician, Lin Halliday, feared that Clark was dying and told Smith that Clark was "one of the best pianists alive and he's killing himself," according to Gilbreath's article. Clark would survive the incident only to die of an overdose eighteen months later at Junior's. Clark was appreciated more overseas than he was at home judging by the sales of his albums. Cool Struttin', for example sold 38,000 copies in this country between 1991 to 2009, while sales in Japan topped 138,000.

Drummer Art Blakey was known not only for his heroin addiction but also for his notorious reputation for introducing heroin to fellow musicians and then firing them when their addiction negatively affected their performance. A.M. Akers, in an article, "Death of a Sidewinder," said Blakey used heroin as currency. "That's the way he paid a lot of guys off. In other words, he gave them drugs, and when it was time to get paid, he took your money." Recording companies had a habit of keeping addicted musicians under contract because they borrowed money against their royalties to buy drugs that they seldom were able to repay, according to the now-defunct Canadian jazz magazine *CODA*.

Saxophonist Gary Bartz of Baltimore, a former heroin addict who played for Blakey with the Jazz Messengers, said Blakey never tried to conceal his addiction. "I was really around it with him because he was loose about it. He'd do it in front of anybody," Bartz related in an interview on drugssexandjazz.blogspot.com.

Blakey admitted he was an addict but avoided talking about introducing heroin to his fellow musicians. "I used to use it," he said in the 1984 interview with the Howard University Jazz Oral History Project.

> *I don't like anything that controls me. Other cats had different weaknesses. I never had to go around and steal because I wasn't a hypocrite. My children protected me. They knew what I was going. I don't like anything that control me, shit, but me. The fun in getting high is not letting people know that you get high. Once they find out, you done lost. I'm so lucky. See, all my family protected me.*

Bartz said his addiction allowed him to meet many great jazz artists who were fellow addicts because "it was more like a community. It was almost like a gang. Guys who were doing it were most visible." He said heroin helped musicians deal with the stress of playing. "It slows everything down so when you're performing…You see everything. You hear everything. You have enough time to make decisions when you're."

Drugs have been synonymous with jazz ever since the end of World War II, when heroin was cheap and plentiful, especially in Pittsburgh's Hill

District night clubs, where dealers trolled nightspots ready to sell heroin to any musician who needed a fix.

Bassist Marcus Kelly of Pittsburgh said he knew musicians who were both drug addicts and alcoholics, and as a bandleader, he was responsible for getting them to engagements on time. "I like to get high but can't you taper it off for a while," he said in an interview with the archives of the African American Jazz Preservation at the University of Pittsburgh.

Kelly recalled times when went to a musician's home and found them strung out on heroin or drunk and in no shape to perform. He had to awaken them, get them dressed, deliver them to a club, pay them, hope they could perform and then take them home afterward. "Business is business. It's enough problems getting a gig without putting up with something like that."

Eldridge Smith, who played the baritone horn, said he knew one musician who drank a half-gallon of wine before a performance and was barely able to play. "Once your head gets clouded up, that's it," said Smith.

Drummer Roger Humphries has been around musicians who were heroin addicts and has witnessed them "nodding" on the bandstand after injecting heroin, he said in an interview with the African American Jazz Preservation Society. "I didn't want to be like that."

A Canadian medical research journal reported in 2009 that cirrhosis of the liver was a common cause of death among jazz musicians because of drug use and chronic alcoholism. The *Canadian Journal of Gastroenterology* cited liver disease as the cause of death for Charlie Parker, John Coltrane, Stan Getz, Ben Webster, Coleman Hawkins and Dexter Gordon—likely caused by their heroin addictions.

Pianist Jerry Kaminsky was well known in Pittsburgh music circles in the 1950s, playing regularly at the Midway Lounge and the Carnival Lounge. The twenty-eight-year-old musician finished an engagement at a nightclub outside Pittsburgh and then died of a heroin overdose in 1956. His father found him dead the next morning still wearing his clothes from the night before. Kaminsky and two other men had been arrested in the Hill District after purchasing heroin, according to the *Pittsburgh Press*. Another paper, the *Post-Gazette*, referred to Kaminsky "as one of the most brilliant young composers"

Charlie Parker became synonymous with jazz and heroin by bringing the drug into the forefront of the jazz culture. Parker, who is credited with introducing bebop, also is credited with inspiring other musicians to experiment with heroin because they believed it could make them play with the intensity and skill that marked Parker's performances.

Dr. Charles Winick, a New York psychologist who conducted interviews of 350 jazz musicians in the 1950s about their drug use, wrote that Parker changed the face of jazz with the introduction of bebop. He said musicians believed they could play better if they used heroin. Musicians, Winick added, turned to heroin to alleviate the boredom of long trips and exhaustion and in the mistaken belief the drug would increase their energy levels.

Dr. Harris B. Stratyer said jazz artists are under the mistaken belief that heroin helps them play more creatively in a 2010 article in *Psychology Today*, "A Myth about Alcohol, Drugs and Creativity." Jazz critic Nat Hentoff, writing in his 1961 book, *Jazz Life*, said that the music "attracted a smaller percentage of emotional adolescents," which made them susceptible to drug use.

> *It's true that much of the freshness and unpredictability of jazz has been due to the fact that, from its beginning, its players set their own pragmatic musical standards. Music school rules of "legitimacy" of tone, for example, were ignored. A man was judged by the quality of his ear, his capacity to improvise and the personal texture of his sound and style. But those flexible criteria also made it possible for musicians with considerable "natural" talent but limited powers of self-discipline (in music or anything else) to make a place for themselves fairly quickly in jazz life. Some blew well, but remained quasi-children all their lives.*

Jazz musicians are considered rebels and outsiders. Winick quoted one musician talking about their unorthodox behavior. "Our rebel instincts broke music away from what I would call the handcuffed and straightjacket discipline of the classical school," the musician said in "The Use of Drugs Among Jazz Musicians" in the journal *Social Problems* in 1959.

The drug helped musicians deal with the boredom of touring, depression, stress and frustration about their work, wrote Dr. Frederick J. Spencer in his book *Jazz and Death. Medical Profiles of Jazz Greats.* Musicians believed heroin helped them play better and also relieved pain of wrist and back injuries sustained during performing. Spencer said jazz artists also suffered from other ailments such as diabetes, lung cancer, alcoholism, eye problems and tuberculosis. Many musicians were born in poverty and also suffered from malnutrition, Spencer wrote.

Pianist Frank Cunimondo said he played with musicians who were heroin addicts and sometimes drove them to the Hill District to get their fix. "They would fall asleep on the bandstand and wake up during the second act," he said in an interview.

The use of heroin by jazz musicians worried officials of Pittsburgh Local 60 of the American Federation of Musicians. Pittsburgh newspapers bannered stories of musicians being arrested in raids at clubs or being nabbed while possessing heroin. Local president Hal Davis was concerned about the union's image and tried to downplay the use of heroin among jazz artists after one of its members was arrested for being part of a heroin ring.

"We are greatly concerned over the adverse publicity," he told the *Pittsburgh Press* in 1956. "The influence would indicate to the general public that all musicians, or a great majority, are habitual users, peddlers or pushers of dope. Nothing could be farther from the truth. A very minute percentage has been addicted."

16

THE FUTURE OF JAZZ

The end of World War II was a boon for jazz in Pittsburgh. The draft depleted the ranks of Pittsburgh jazz musicians, but by 1945 newly discharged artists had picked up where they left off before the war by joining bands and forming new groups to perform for a jazz-hungry city. Gas rationing was lifted, and alcohol was plentiful. Nightclubs were filled. Restrictions on the purchase of building materials was lifted by 1947, and clubs spruced up their appearances by remodeling and increasing the size of their entertainment budgets. Floor shows once again were popular. Big-name acts like Mary Lou Williams, Erroll Garner and Roy Eldridge continued to appear in Pittsburgh clubs. Norman Granz' Jazz at the Philharmonic continued to pack the Syria Mosque.

Pittsburgh City Council passed a measure allowing clubs to stay open until 2:00 a.m., and the *Pittsburgh Post-Gazette* reported in 1946 that liquor license applications soared. By 1946, there were 1,333 licensed drinking spots in the city along with 283 after-hours clubs. There were more than 1,600 liquor licenses in Allegheny County.

Then musical tastes changed. Swing music, popular during the war years, gave way to bebop, and people stopped listening to jazz because bebop was harder to dance to with its faster tempos and more complex melodies. By the mid-1950s, rock 'n' roll had arrived, further diminishing interest in jazz.

The size of jazz audiences nationwide at clubs and concerts declined and has continued to drop. Attendance at jazz performances decreased to nearly 15 percent in 2008 from more than 19 percent in 1982, according to the

Erroll Garner publicity photo. *Erroll Garner Archive. University of Pittsburgh Library System.*

Jazz Audiences Initiative which conducted a survey of nineteen cities and thirteen universities in 2010. The analysis found that the jazz audience also was getting older, with a median age of forty-nine years compared to twenty-nine years in 1982.

Technology is also changing the way music is presented to listeners. Ever since pianists learned to play by using piano rolls, computers, software and electronic instruments are changing the face of jazz, wrote Ted Gioia, a jazz historian and critic, in "Jazz Composition in the Digital Age" for the American Society of Composers, Authors and Publishers:

> *The rise of microphones in the 1920s allowed for a new intimacy in jazz performance, and the Golden Age of American Song…might never have happened without this breakthrough. The advent of the long-playing album in the 1950s opened up the door for extended jazz compositions. The availability of affordable synthesizers changed the rulebook again in the 1970s, and the rise of web-based technologies did the same in the 1990s. That last revolution may be the most disruptive and long-lasting. And the digital world impacts more than just the construction of the music—it has also changed distribution, dissemination, remuneration, and virtually every other aspect of the life of the musical work after it has been composed. Not since the birth of the recording industry has the making of music been so inexorably altered.*

Saxophonist Don Aliquo Sr., who is in his nineties and continues to perform, said jazz continues to evolve—although he is not optimistic that it will ever regain the popularity it once had despite advances in technology. He said some contemporary artists in Pittsburgh are experimenting with free jazz, which follows no musical rules, follows no harmonic structure, has no fixed tempo and changes chords at will.

"Most of it is terrible because they don't know how to do it yet." Aliquo said in an interview, "The current jazz scene, he added, is too commercial. "It's commercial jazz. It's middle of the road. Jazz is a bottomless pit. There's so much that passes for jazz."

Then there is the question of how musicians will be paid. Artists are struggling financially, Aliquo said. Some musicians, in order to get exposure, pay a club owner for a percentage of the door to allow them to perform. "Some just play for the door. They don't even get a guarantee," he added.

Despite the pessimism, other musicians are optimistic about the future of the music. "Modern jazz will never die," said guitarist Joe Negri. "It might come back in a different form."

BIBLIOGRAPHY

Newspapers

Gazette Times
Missouri Herald
New York Age
New York Times
Paducah Evening Sun
Pittsburgh Courier
Pittsburgh Gazette
Pittsburgh Post
Pittsburgh Post-Gazette
Pittsburgh Press
Pittsburgh Sun-Telegraph
Pittsburgh Weekly Gazette
Rock Island Argus
Wilkes-Barre News Leader

Archives

African American Jazz Preservation Society of Pittsburgh Oral History Project, 1995–1999, AIS.1998.04, Archives & Special Collections, University of Pittsburgh Library System.

American Civil Liberties Union Papers, 1974–76 Legal Case Files, Racial Discrimination, Item 582, Mudd Library, Princeton University.

American Federation of Musicians, Local 60-471, Pittsburgh, Pa. Records, 1906–1996, AIS.1997.41, Archives & Special Collections, University of Pittsburgh Library System.

Erroll Garner Archive, 1942–2010, AIS.2015.09. Archives and Special Collections, University of Pittsburgh Library System.

Howard University Jazz Oral History Project.

Martha Glaser Papers, 1921–2010, AIS.2015.09 Archives and Special Collections, University of Pittsburgh Library System.

Maurice Levy Oral History of Music in Pittsburgh, Carnegie Library, Pittsburgh.

MCG Jazz Archives, MCG Jazz/Smithsonian Institute, Pittsburgh Jazz Legends Oral Histories.

National Museum of American History, Jazz Oral History Collection, 1988–1990.

Pittsburgh and Beyond: The Experience of the Jewish Community. National Council of Jewish Women, Pittsburgh Section, Oral History Collection, University of Pittsburgh.

Records of the American Federation of Musicians of Music Local 471, Pittsburgh, Pa. 1906–1996, Archives and Special Collections, University of Pittsburgh Library System.

"The Roots of the African American Musicians' Union Local No. 471 of the American Federation of Musicians in the City of Pittsburgh 1920-1966 and Beyond." AIS, 1998.04, University of Pittsburgh Labor Archives. Archives of Industrial Society.

Smithsonian Jazz Oral History Program, 1988–1990.

Wilma Dobie Papers and Sound Recordings, Institute of Jazz Studies, Rutgers University Libraries.

Books

Balliett, Whitney. *American Musicians: 56 Portraits in Jazz*. New York: Oxford University Press, 1986.

Barry, John M. *Rising Tide: The Great Mississippi Flood of 1927 and How It Changed America*. New York: Simon & Schuster, 1997.

Bergreen, Laurence. *Louis Armstrong: An Extravagant Life*. New York: Broadway Books, 1997.

Boucher, John Newton. *A Century and a Half of Pittsburgh People*. Pittsburgh: Lewis Publishing Company, 1908.

Brewer, John, Jr. *African Americans in Pittsburgh*. Charleston, SC: Arcadia Publishing, 2006.

———. *Pittsburgh Jazz*. Charleston, SC: Arcadia Publishing, 2007.

Buck, Solon J., and Elizabeth Buck. *The Planting of Civilization in Western Pennsylvania*. Pittsburgh: University of Pittsburgh Press, 1939.

Buckley, Gail Lumet. *The Hornes: An American Family*. New York: Alfred A. Knopf, 1986.

Buerkle, Jack V., and Danny Barber. *Bourbon Street Black: The New Orleans Black Jazzman*. New York: Oxford University Press, 1973.

Buni, Andrew. *Robert L. Vann of the Pittsburgh Courier: Politics and Black Journalism*. Pittsburgh: University of Pittsburgh Press, 1974.

Caldwell, Erskine. *Tenant Farmer*. New York: Phalanx Press, 1935.

Conner, Lynne. *Pittsburgh in Stages: Two Hundred Years of Theater*. Pittsburgh: University of Pittsburgh Press, 2007.

Crow, Bill. *Jazz Anecdotes*. New York: Oxford University Press, 2005.

Doran, James M. *The Most Happy Piano*. Metuchen, NJ: Scarecrow Press and the Institute of Jazz Studies, Rutgers University, 1985.

Fernett, Gene. *Swing Out: Great Negro Dance Bands*. Cocoa, FL: Pendell Publishing, 1967.

Foner, Eric. *Reconstruction: America's Unfinished Revolution, 1863–1877*. New York: History Book Club, 1988.

Gates, Henry Louis, Jr. *Stony the Road: Reconstruction, White Supremacy, and the Rise of Jim Crow*. New York: Penguin Press, 2019.

George, Kathleen. *The Blues Walked In*. Pittsburgh: University of Pittsburgh Press, 2018.

Gioia, Ted. *History of Jazz*. New York: Oxford University Press, 2011.

Glasco, Laurence A. "Double Burden: The Black Experience in Pittsburgh." In *City at the Point: Essays on the Social History of Pittsburgh*, edited by Samuel P. Hays, 69–109. Pittsburgh: University of Pittsburgh Press, 2010.

Glasco, Laurence A., ed. *The WPA History of the Negro in Pittsburgh*. Pittsburgh: University of Pittsburgh Press, 2004.

Glasco, Laurence A., and Christopher Rawson. *August Wilson: Pittsburgh Places in His Life and Plays*. Pittsburgh: Pittsburgh History and Landmarks Foundation, 2011.

Goodrich, Dave. *Key to the City: A Guide to Pittsburgh Music History, Entertainment and More*. N.p.: self-published, 1985.

Gottlieb, Peter. *Making Their Own Way: Southern Black Migration to Pittsburgh, 1916–1930*. Urbana: University of Illinois Press, 1997.

Gottlieb, Robert, ed. *Reading Jazz: A Gathering of Autobiography, Reportage and Criticism from 1919 to Now*. New York: Knopf Doubleday Publishing, 1996.

Gregory, James N. *The Southern Diaspora: How the Great Migration of Black and White Southerners Transformed America*. Chapel Hill: University of North Carolina Press, 2005.

Hadju, David. *Lush Life: A Biography of Billy Strayhorn*. New York: North Point Press, 1996.

Hays, Samuel P. *City at the Point: Essays on the Social History of Pittsburgh*. Pittsburgh: University of Pittsburgh Press, 1989.

Jenkins, Philip. *Hoods and Shirts: The Extreme Right in Pennsylvania, 1925–1950*. Chapel Hill: University of North Carolina Press, 1997.

Kenney, William Howland. *Jazz on the River*. Chicago: University of Chicago Press, 2005.

Leman, Nichols. *The Promised Land: The Great Black Migration and How It Changed America*. New York: Vintage Books, 1991.

Litwack, Lon F. *Trouble in Mind: Black Southerners in the Age of Jim Crow*. New York: Alfred A. Knopf, 1999.

Lorant, Stefan. *Pittsburgh: The Story of an American City*. Pittsburgh: Esselmont Books, 1999.

Martinez, J. Michael. *A Long Dark Night: Race in America from Jim Crow to World War II*. Lanham, MD: Rowman & Littlefield, 2006.

Owsley, Dennis. *City of Gabriels: The History of Jazz in St. Louis, 1895–1933*. St. Louis, MO: Reedy Press, 2006.

Palmer, Rob. *Mr. P.C.: The Life and Music of Paul Chambers*. Sheffield, UK: Equinox Publishing, 2012.

Peretti, Burton W. *The Creation of Jazz: Music, Race and Culture in Urban America*. Urbana: University of Illinois Press, 1992.

Pitch, Anthony S. *The Last Lynching: How a Gruesome Murder Rocked a Small Georgia Town*. New York: Skyhorse Publishing, 2016.

Razlogova, Elena. *The Listener's Voice: Early Radio and the American Public*. Philadelphia: University of Pennsylvania Press, 2011.

Rosengarten, Theodore. *Tombee: Portrait of a Cotton Planter*. New York: William Morrow, 1986.

Scott, Emmett J., ed. "Letters of Negro Migrants 1916–1918." *Journal of Negro History* 4, no. 3 (July 1919): 290–340.

Shipton, Alyn. *A New History of Jazz: Revised and Updated*. 2nd ed. New York: Continuum International Publishing Group, 2007.

Spencer, Dr. Frederick J. *Jazz and Death. Medical Profiles of Jazz Greats*. Biloxi: University of Mississippi Press, 2002.

Sultanoff, Jeff. *Experiencing Big Band Jazz*. Lanham, MD: Rowman & Littlefield, 2017.

Taylor, Hosea. *Dirt Street*. Pittsburgh: Arsenal Binding & Finishing, 2007.

Trotter, Joe W., and Jared Day. *Race and Renaissance: African Americans in Pittsburgh Since World War II*. Pittsburgh: University of Pittsburgh Press, 2010.

Turner, Helen A. *The Negroes in Pittsburgh, in Wage-Earning Pittsburgh: The Pittsburgh Survey*. ed., Paul Underwood. Kellogg, NY: Survey Associates, 1914.

Tye, Larry. *Rising from the Rails: Pullman Porters and the Making of the Black Middle Class*. New York: Henry Holt and Company, 2004.

Ward, Geoffrey C., and Ken Burns. *Jazz: A History of America's Music*. New York: Alfred A. Knopf, 2005.

Whitaker, Mark. *Smoketown: The Untold Story of the Other Great Black Renaissance*. New York: Simon & Schuster, 2019.

Wilkerson, Isabel. *The Warmth of Other Suns: The Epic Story of America's Great Migration*. New York: Vintage Books, 2010.

Woodson, Carter G. *A Century of Negro Migration*. Washington, D.C.: Association for the Study of Negro Life and History, 1918.

Government Reports

Historic American Building Survey, Library of Congress, loc.gov HABS no. Pa. 6780.

Negro Migration 1916–17. Washington, D.C.: U.S. Department of Labor, Committee on Education and Labor, 1919.

Report of the Committee of the Senate on the Relations Between Labor and Capital. Forty-Eighth Congress, 1885.

Court Cases

Black Musicians of Pittsburgh v. Local 60-471, AFM, AFL-CIO, October 21, 1971, 375 F. supp 902 (W.D. Pa. 1974).

Black Musicians of Pittsburgh, et al v. Local 60-471 American Federation of Musicians, AFL-CIO, 75-2244.

BMOP and George Childress, Rubye Younge, DeRuyther Kemp, Thomas Miller, Charles Austin and George Spaulding and EEOC v. Local 471-AFM, AFL-CIO, 71-1008.

Articles

Adler, David R. "Jeff 'Tain' Watts; How He Revolutionized Jazz Drumming." *Jazztimes*, November 20, 2015.

Akers, A.H. "Death of a Sidewinder." Narratively, narratively.com.

Anderson, George. "Frances Turk Buries Her Son." *Pittsburgh Post-Gazette*, August 18, 1981.

Barbour, George. "'New Hill' Will Erase Landmarks." *Pittsburgh Courier*, April 20, 1963.

———. "URA in Clash on Hill Project." *Pittsburgh Courier*, June 13, 1964.

———. "Word on Lower Hill: Say Goodbye Next Spring." *Pittsburgh Courier*, August 27, 1955

Bernabo, David. "The Search for the Pittsburgh Sound." Medium, medium.com. August 11, 2017.

Bishop, Pete. "She's Come Home to Sing and Sup." *Pittsburgh Press*, March 6, 1980.

Bradford, Gary. "They Labor for the Love of Jazz." *Pittsburgh Press*, October 19, 1980.

Butler, Ann. "Birdie's Place." *Pittsburgh Press*, April 3, 1984.

———. "Sophie." *Pittsburgh Press*, January 18, 1988.

Byrd, Jerry. "Heyday of the Hill." *Pittsburgh Press*, March 1, 1987.

Cohen, Harold V. "The Drama Desk." *Pittsburgh Post-Gazette*, February 15, 1947.

Dorman, John L. "August Wilson's Pittsburgh." *New York Times*, August 15, 2017.

Epstein, Abraham. "The Negro Migrant in Pittsburgh." University of Pittsburgh, School of Economics, 1918.

Eskey, Kenneth. "Lower Hill Proposals Unveiled." *Pittsburgh Press*, June 4, 1959.

Gaul, Harvey B. "Charleston Negroes Primitive and Picturesque as Report on South Atlantic Coast." *Pittsburgh Post*, May 8, 1921.

Guidry, Nate. "Chuck Austin, The 'Perfect Sideman' Raises the Bar for Career Jazz Players." *Pittsburgh Post-Gazette*, July 11, 2004.

Harmetz, Alljean. "Lena Horne, Singer and Actress, Dies at 92." *New York Times*, May 10, 2010.

Kalina, Mike. "The Piano Ladies." *Pittsburgh Post-Gazette*, June 8, 1978.

Kalson, Sally. "Once a Hotbed of Jazz." *Pittsburgh Post-Gazette*, February 26, 1988.

Krug, Karl. "Show Stops." *Pittsburgh Post-Gazette*, June 20, 1930.

Leonard, Vince. "44 Years of Jaynes' Jazz." *Pittsburgh Post-Gazette*, Jan. 27, 1983.

Lillis, Karen. "Passing Through: A Haphazard History of Pittsburgh Hotels." The Glassblock, theglassblock.com. August 23, 2016.

Martin, Douglas. "Ray Brown, Master Jazz Bassist, Dies at 75." *New York Times*, July 4, 2002.

McClendon, Lisa, "Where Is Jazz? Pittsburgh Musicians Speak of the Changing Times." *Pittsburgh Courier*, January 10, 1998.

McIntire, Burt. "Pittsburgh Churches Hold Finest of Musical Services." *Pittsburgh Press*, September 5, 1924.

Musick, Phil. "Birdie Caused a Lot of Joy and Jazz at Old Hurricane." *Pittsburgh Press*, November 11, 1984.

New York Times. "Fate Marable." January 19, 1947.

———. "To Suppress Jazz Dancing; Pittsburgh Dance Hall Proprietors Will Probably Ask a City Ordinance." February 4, 1920.

O'Neill, Pat. "Shafer Here Today to Tour Hill District." *Pittsburgh Post-Gazette*, September 15, 1966.

O'Toole, Christine. "Pittsburgh Pursues Plan to Demolish the 'Igloo'." *New York Times*, March 8, 2011.

Paducah Evening Sun. "Colored School Commencement." May 20, 1907.

———. "Colored Schools Will Entertain." May 27, 1907.

Perry, Diana. "Hill District Doomed?" *Pittsburgh Courier*, November 21, 1971.

Pittsburgh Courier. "Bill to Build Sports Arena in Hill Introduced." April 11, 1953.

———. "Desertion Charged in Lena Horne Divorce Suit." February 15, 1941.

———. "Fate Marable, 56, Dies in St. Louis." January 25, 1947.

———. "Good Old Days." September 22, 1990.

———. "Lena Horne, Hubby, 'Make-Up.' Café Society Star Joins Louis Jones in Pittsburgh." October 25, 1944.

———. "Refuses to Appear at Premiere of Own Film." June 18, 1938.

———. "Says Hill Must Be Destroyed." February 25, 1950.

———. "Secret's Out: Lena Horne's Married." June 25, 1950.

———. "'We Want No Black Babies,' Says Police Chief." July 23, 1938.

Pittsburgh Post. "Council Orders Rook to Put End to Police Brutality," June 25, 1925.

———. "Jazz Is Sin. It Is Barbaric Music." October 31, 1921.

———. "More Officers Sent to Guard Stowe Negroes from Attack." November 12, 1923.

———. "Negroes Comply with Stowe Twp. Orders to Move." October 10, 1923.

———. "Nothing but Jazz! Jazz! Jazz!" October 8, 1930.

———. "Stowe Township Negroes Order to Leave Community." October 10, 1923.

Pittsburgh Weekly Gazette. "Peter DeClary." January 26, 1808.

Rosenblum, Charles. "In the Hill, a Fabulous Jazz Landmark Is Virtually Reborn." *Pittsburgh City Paper*, August 9, 2007.

Rosensweet, Alvin. "Housing 'Riot' Predicted Here Months Ago." *Pittsburgh Post-Gazette*, September 15, 1966.

Schacht, Beulah. "Story of Fate Marable." Doctor Jazz, doctorjazz.co.uk.

Seidenberg, Mel. "Lower Hill Building Plans Set." *Pittsburgh Post-Gazette*, August 13, 1959.

———. "Lower Hill Families Benefit by Relocation." *Pittsburgh Post-Gazette*, June 6, 1959.

Sprigle, Ray. "8,000 Jammed in Tumble-Down Rookeries in City's Hill District." *Pittsburgh Post-Gazette*, April 16, 1954.

———. "The Law Just Doesn't Worry Much About What Happens on the Hill." *Pittsburgh Post-Gazette*, April 20, 1954.

Taylor, Robert. "Big Projects Explosive Issue in City View and Henger Street." *Pittsburgh Press*, September 24, 1950.

Washington, Chester. "The Avenue: Reflections from Wylie the Street that Starts at a Church and Ends in a Jail." *Pittsburgh Courier*, January 14, 1939.

Wilson, John S. "Erroll Garner, 53; Composed 'Misty', 'That's My Kick'." *New York Times*, January 3, 1977.

Zurowski, Ann. "Champion of Music." *Pittsburgh Press*, January 8, 1961.

Theses and Dissertations

Carter, Janelle R. "From Their Own Voice: The Lived Experience of African Americans Exposed to Jim Crow." PhD diss., Duquesne University, 2015.

Farley, Jeff, "Making America's Music: Jazz History and the Jazz Preservation Act." PhD diss., University of Glasgow, 2008.

Harper, Colter. "The Crossroads of the World; A Social and Cultural History of Jazz in Pittsburgh's Hill District, 1920–1970." PhD diss., University of Pittsburgh, 2011.

Johnson, Lulamae, "Development of African American Gospel Piano Style, 1926–1960: A Socio-economic Analysis of Arizona Dranes and Thomas A. Dorse." PhD diss., University of Pittsburgh, 2009.

Mackey, Michael Paul. "From Pittsburgh to the Pershing: Orchestration, Interaction and Influence in the Early Work of Ahmad Jamal." PhD diss., University of Pittsburgh, 2017.

Pena, Carlos, E. "Pittsburgh Jazz Records and Beyond, 1950–1985." Master's thesis, University of Pittsburgh, 2007.

Stocking, Collis A. "Study of Dance Halls in Pittsburgh." Pittsburgh Girls' Conference, 1925.

Taylor, William E. "The Vision and Development of Jazz Piano: A New Perspective for Educators." PhD diss., University of Massachusetts–Amherst, 1975.

Films

MCG Jazz Archives. *We Knew What We Had: The Greatest Jazz Story Never Told.* 2018.

Wylie Avenue Days. WQED Media, 2007. Producers Doug Bolin and Christopher Moore. Exec. producer Nancy Lavin.

Journal Articles

Adams, Paul. "The Lost Years: The Impact of Cirrhosis on the History of Jazz." *Canadian Journal of Gastroenterology* 23, no. 6 (June 2009): 405–6.

Baynham, Edward G. "Henry Kleber, Early Pittsburgh Musician." *Western Pennsylvania History*, September–December, 1942.

Campbell, Paulette. "Documenting Pittsburgh's Past." *Magazine of the National Endowment for the Humanities*, March–April 2005.

Doyle, Patrick. "Pittsburg's Hill District Reimagined." *Pittsburgh Magazine*, January 22, 2015.

Gilbreath, Aaron. "The Lost Footage of Pianist Sonny Clark." *Michigan Quarterly Review*, March 17, 2016.

Gioia, Ted. "How New York City Became the Epicenter of Jazz." *City Journal*, September 9, 2016.

Glasco, Larry. "The 1940s. The Best of Times." *Western Pennsylvania History*, Spring 2015.

Gorczyca, Robert. "Chuck Austin: Musician with a Mission." *Western Pennsylvania History*, Summer 2017.

Harpster, John W. "Eighteenth-Century Inns and Taverns of Western Pennsylvania." *Western Pennsylvania History*, March 1936.

Hentoff, Nat. "Jazz and Jim Crow." *The Commonweal*, March 24, 1961.

Kemp, Kathryn. "When Gospel Music Sparked a Worship War." *Christianity Today*, December 7, 2018.

McDevitt, Bette. "Show Stoppers: When Local Women Entertained Pittsburgh Audiences." *Western Pennsylvania History*, Summer 2004.

Reid, Ira De. A. "The Social Condition of the Negro in the Hill District of Pittsburgh." General Committee of the Hill Survey, 1930.

Richman, Hyman. "Life on Pittsburgh's Hill: Some Views and Values of Jews Who Lived There Before the 1940s." *Pittsburgh History*, Spring 1991.

Sewald, Jeff. "Ahmad Jamal, Jazz Master." *Pittsburgh Quarterly*, Fall 2017.

Simms, Margaret, Marla McDaniel, Saunji D. Fyffe and Christopher Lowenstein. "Structural Barriers to Racial Equality in Pittsburgh." Urban Institute, October 2015.

Smith, Scott, and Steven Manaker. "Pittsburgh's African-American Neighborhoods, 1900–1920." *Pittsburgh History,* Winter 1995–1996.

Trotter, Joe W. "Reflections on the Great Migration to Western Pennsylvania." *Pittsburgh History*, Winter, 1994–95.

Winick, Charles Dr. "The Use of Drugs by Jazz Musicians." *Social Problem* 78, no. 4 (Winter 1995–96).

Woodson, Carter D., and Emmett J. Scott. "Letters of Negro Migrants of 1916–1918" *Journal of Negro History* 4, no. 3 (July 1919).

ABOUT THE AUTHORS

RICHARD GAZARIK is journalist and author. He has won awards for his writing and investigative reporting into public and corporate corruption in Pennsylvania. He is the author of *Black Valley: The Life and Death of Fannie Sellins*, *Prohibition Pittsburgh* and *Wicked Pittsburgh*, both published by The History Press, and the biography, *The Mayor of Shantytown: The Life of Father James Renshaw Cox.*

KAREN ANTHONY COLE is a lifetime musician and music educator in Western Pennsylvania. She is a retired high school band director where she taught and mentored students in marching, symphonic, jazz band and jazz history electives. She has directed various ensembles and is a performing member of local college and community bands. Karen is a graduate of Edinboro University of Pennsylvania.